Original Love

2.20.
Sweet Andi,
It's here—
Listen—
you know—
Love, Nadia

Original Love

FIND LOVE. LIVE LOVE. SHARE LOVE.

Nadia Khalil Bradley

THREE CORNERS
PRESS
SAN MARINO, CALIFORNIA

THREE CORNERS PRESS

Three Corners Press
P O Box 80264
San Marino, CA 91118-0264

Publishers Cataloging-in-Publication

Bradley, Nadia Khalil

Original Love / Nadia Khalil Bradley. - 1st ed. - San Marino, CA:
Three Corners Press, 2013.

p. ; cm.
ISBN: 978-0-9755585-1-5
Summary: A collection of timeless wisdom that provides practical guidance and thought-provoking questions that will enable you to find, live and share the Original Love with which you came to Earth.

1. Poetry. 2. Spiritual life. 3. Etc.

BT966.3 .B73 2011 2011903975
235.3-dc22 0709

Editor	Susan Gilchrist Navas
Book Cover	Marilu Diaz / Dawn Katzin
Interior Design	Marilu Diaz
Copywriting	Linda Papciak

This book is dedicated to the love of our very own souls.

To keep love alive is our job
To feel it, to live in it, to carry it, to share it.

Contents

Love

The Quiet Peace of Love

We think of love as fireworks
Or sheer joy, or pain
Or happiness beyond belief

And as life grows us
We find that love is content
It is quiet
Its actions are felt
And its words are few

There is not a word that describes a tear
Or a look in a person's eye
There is no word for the happiness that we feel
It is just a sigh, a smile, enjoyment of its grandness
There is simply a quiet peace to love

We expect so much from love
That we forget it is a feeling
We want so much from love
That at times we don't hear what it is trying to tell us

And all love has to say is
I love you as you are
You don't need to be anything
You just need to know
That whatever you have inside of you
You have for a reason

Let what is inside of you live
Clean it up if you need to
Do it with passion

Life is just the vehicle
For the work you came to do
Your body is the way to do it
And your soul is your guide

We spend so much time telling life what to do
That we forget
That we are not here to control life
Life is learning
To allow life to teach us

Love along the Way

The person who waits for you to redeem yourself
Knowing it will redeem them too

The one who opens a door for you
As though they are touching your integrity

The driver who does not cut in front of you
Who reminds you that you are that person too

The person who says it's okay
It was not meant for you

The friend that says you are really good at this
And you grow it as a treasured thought

The person who stops walking or talking
When you say I love you
And says I love you too

We are all each other
And when love is there
We get to feel a part of each other
We carry each other in ourselves
And when the days may not answer all of our questions
We remember the smile, the trust, the treasured thoughts

The soul who gives us the tools to say
I am still okay, I am the same person who woke up yesterday
And today I have this challenge
I know this will pass

I may find out in all of this
That today is the seed that grows my direction
I am already meant to be here or I wouldn't be
And while I am here I am accomplishing my desires
And at times it will look hard
At times it will be soft and easy

The love that comes to me
Is the love the teaches me and moves me
Love is the trail of every soul's thoughts
And when it is felt, it is the warm blanket

So allow love to show you
Accept love to feel it
Receive love so that you know the value of sharing it
Share love and it is the lover of love

We Love Love

Isn't it great when you hear something nice about yourself
A smile moves from your heart to your face
And you think of those nice words you heard
While you're driving, shopping, eating or ready to fall asleep
You think of how great it is to feel loved

We know how to love others so easily
We love to love
And when we hear or feel another's love of us
We give them a part of us
Because we cannot help but love when we are loved

Imagine if on Earth
We noticed how we love
How we love to feel love for others
No matter who they are
Or what they do

It relieves us of wariness, doubt, and skepticism
It relieves us of thinking we cannot trust or share with them
It makes us want to listen
And to give back
As you feel the lightness of being part of another person

We often think that people are too much work
And that you cannot trust anyone
But then we miss the beauty we could find along the way

The quiet people who do not speak
Have life breathed into them when they are spoken to
When they are smiled at
They smile back without thought

When we are noticed
We try to live up to what we were noticed for
We can be the person who speaks kind words
We can share a positive thought when we think it

So say something
It really does make a difference
And it really does make us better people

Never underestimate the power of sharing and kindness
It is the juicy burger
The great play
The beautiful flower
The song we sing all day
It is the warm popcorn that once you smell it
You have to have some
It is the sunshine of our souls

So Simple is Love

So simple is love that it actually tells you what to do
It can't help itself
You smile without thinking
You do kind things without saying why
You ask questions without feeling like you can't
And you don't feel burdened by anything

Whenever you feel good you are feeling love
If you know that, you have a map
Of where to go to find it in your thoughts, your choices

We think love comes to us in the form of a person
But love is so much more, it is about feeling loved
All by yourself
To know that the origin of love is in you

And when you know that
It lightens your workload
You feel safe, wanted, and appreciated
Feeling loved does so much for us
That when we feel it we search for it again
And we forget that simply feeling love is important

Sometimes we just have it all backwards
We wait to feel it
And we miss the love that is already around us

If we look around at our lives
And notice those we love who love us back
And the times in each day that are pleasant
And we know that all of it counts
We are living in love

Just One I Love You

We believe people are okay the way they are
But there are things in life that make us better

One smile really does change someone's day
One I love you is never forgotten
And a pat on the back is felt forever

When someone says I love you
And means it
It finds a way of imprinting itself on our hearts
And we hear it over and over again in our heads
It carries us like the weightless energy that keeps us going
It reminds us that when something doesn't work out
That many other things do

It changes our point of view
From nobody loves me
To somebody said they did
And we feel it
It tells us that we are not alone in this world
Because we really don't want to be
We want to be with everyone else
And a part of everyone

That one "I love you"
Does all of that for us
So hungry are our souls
For the simple acts of kindness
And how we appreciate being alive when we receive them

Heartmaker Icebreaker

Sometimes we don't speak to each other
Because we don't know what to say
We think we have to say something important or clever

Yet a simple hello would do
Then the other person can tell you things
And then you can tell them things

We don't have to be preoccupied with what to say
Interest in others is most engaging
Sharing ourselves is what we are really looking for

Sometimes we are so consumed with ourselves
That we don't step outside of our minds
To see that others have so much to offer

We are so worried about what someone else thinks that we can't just relax and speak

We assume so much
We don't have a chance to find out the truth
That others are the same as us
If we heard each other's thoughts we would know
That they are as vulnerable as we are
No matter how differently we see them

Our assumptions are rarely accurate
When it comes to feelings and emotions
Yet if we relied on what we feel
Before we have time to think about it
We would often assume less and know more

We all came here to teach each other
Yet we have found ways to do everything ourselves
We fear needing each other
But we don't want to be alone either
And we don't really know how to break the ice

It is the interest and the attention you give
No matter what words are used
That bridges the gaps between us

A simple hello, a smile, a nod
Tomorrow you can say more
And the next day we can ask how it all went
And the next we can say let's get a bite to eat

We will grow circles of love
And believe there is more good in the world
Than we thought the day before
All with a simple, what's up?

Sustainable Love

We expect so much from love
We want it to make us happy
We want it to take care of the rest of our lives
When and if it comes
Love is always here
Yet it doesn't recognize itself
With all of the conditions we place on it
He or she is love if they meet my expectations
It is love if it makes me look good
It is love if it's what I wanted

We don't even let love surprise us anymore
When a person tells us they love us
We don't believe them
And continue treating them as though they don't
We respect those who don't love
Thinking it is just business,
Or they are doing what they have to do
As if there are certain times and places for love

We don't respect those who love us
Because we can't figure out why they do
If we don't feel love for ourselves, why should they?

We hear about living in the moment
Why is it so important?
Think about where love is
It isn't yesterday or tomorrow
It isn't in the next goal attained or the next relationship
Or when certain conditions are met

Love may be there
But the "there" will only be when it's "here"
Now, in this moment
If we wait, it will never come
If we look, we will never find it

Try loving where you are
As if where you are is perfect
Love your job, don't wait for a better one
Love your partner, even if you disagree
Love your children when they disappoint you
Love yourself when you are alone

Love is the challenge of our soul's discovery
Love is not winning or losing
Getting or not having
Needing or wanting

Life is just a series of moments
Look at those you love and remember why you do
When the "right" person shows up
Or the "right" opportunity presents itself
You will be the same then as you are in this moment

Love isn't postponed
It isn't based on conditions
Do you really think the grass is greener elsewhere?
The grass is already green and if you can't see that now
You never will
No matter whose grass you're standing on

Love is a state of mind
Love is a way of being
Love is what we choose
Love is never a chore

It is time to let love be what it is
A healer of us
The natural medicine of our souls
The glue that bonds us together

And love doesn't disappear, we disappear

If we can just say yes to living in our moments
It will slow us down from searching
To find what we are standing in front of
And it will allow us to see future love when it arrives
It will give us more to share
And the rewards are ours

Understanding love in this way
Can only attract love to you
It is called recognition

Love Anytime

There is no time for when
There is no way for how
There is no reason to do it
Just love in this minute

Love when you talk or don't talk
Love when you solve or walk away until you can
Love when you cook and it will taste better
Love when you shop and you will buy things you love
Love when you eat and you will eat slowly and be satisfied

Love is so simple
That we walk right past the love of ourselves
And the love of others
On our way to love
As though it is an obscure thing
When it is a simple thing
So easy to smile into
And walk around with
So you can look the world in the eye
And it can smile right back at you

You can never learn too much when it comes to love
Love really is endless
Love doesn't have to look a certain way
Or be a certain way
All you have to do is feel it

Feel it and let it feel you
Say it and let it live around you
Think it and it will come out in your words

Dream it and it will walk into your days

Think Love to Create Love

Love starts to teach you who you are
When you think of sharing your home and your heart
It tells you the best of you
Is within you

Love is not a fantasy
And only reality when you find it
That is the excitement of it all

When you think of love
Notice how your thoughts are kind
Full of compassion and understanding
And you smile

Some of us wait for new love to feel such feelings
As though it is the only way we can feel it
You can feel this on your own
Love is love in all places

There isn't one kind of love
Love is in everything

The feeling of presenting yourself to someone new
Is already present
As you build your life with love for yourself
The truth of you emerges
And it attracts the same to you

Love is a part of every day
We are attracted to those who feel their love
We see them as safe, kind, happy

We see it in young children, elders, pets
And those who show love with daily kindness

When you feel it you notice you are different
You believe you are deserving of love

You need only feel it in your heart
The voice of ego disappears
You feel humble and gracious

Knowing love doesn't eliminate challenges
It just makes them easier to face
If you give yourself a break
Love tells you you're okay no matter what

Love finds a way to say yes
To life, to sharing, to understanding
Love is the smile on your face
And the truth of why we are here
To teach us to let go
Enough to open our hearts
To follow its flow
And see where it takes us

Can You Handle Love?

What happens when you feel like you are loved too much?
Can you handle it?
Do you feel you deserve it?
Do you take advantage of it?
Do you enjoy it?
Are you able to live in the moment of it?

Children assume they are loved already
So they run around and play happily
They don't worry whether or not someone loves them
Until we teach them to

They run up to hug you
They kiss you if they feel like it
They never think about what you will think
Or how you will react
Or worry that you won't kiss them back

We have a lot to learn from truth
The child teaches us
To live in what we feel
Without thinking about it

They are your guide
They love you no matter what you do
And even when you are not nice
They find a way to tell you they still love you

Love is always present in us
Yet we shape it with our experiences
If you weren't shown love when you were young
It becomes harder to accept love from others
Remember that you were that child

Remind yourself of when you were free with love
Before you changed your love

Whatever made you conscious of love
Was someone else's idea of it
And it is theirs, not yours

So love like a child
And need nothing back
When love comes to you
Accept it without reservation
Simply run and play again

We are all children in older bodies
When we try to act cool, we are not being ourselves
Love is being ourselves
We don't need to save it for the "right" people
Everyone needs love, everyone loves love
And everyone enjoys love
Enjoy the moment and what comes next will be a surprise

The chance of love
Is any chance we take
Love's hand is always open
As open as the child who doesn't know anything different

Gimme Some Sugah!

We always just want to feel love
Who we love to see
What we love to do
Loving our work
Our kids
Our friends

And then there's Valentine's Day
A day we have set aside to express love
To show what love looks like to us

So we buy flowers
Red ones mean love
We have towels, tablecloths, and flags with hearts on them
Some of us get engaged on this day for added meaning
We try to love more on this day
Or show it more
Or remind ourselves that we love

What would I love most on Valentine's Day?
I would love the promises of heart
The kind that remind you
You will always be loved no matter what day it is
That when I feel down
You know it has nothing to do with you
And you love me anyway
And give me time to come up for air

That you tell me I am still okay when you're mad at me
So that the next time isn't so severe
And you trust we will grow through anything

I would love if you loved how I look in the morning
And it is what you love most about me
That you love the things about me
That are hidden from the rest of the world
That you love when I am trying and learning

We all really just love love
When we don't feel loved we want to sit quietly
And ask ourselves why are we not loved?
And when we feel loved our souls join us together
The security we need to get past the do you love me?

Just love me
As I love you
No more questions of how or why
Just what do you want to do today?
What movie do you want to see?
What'll we have for dinner?
I just want you to be with me

Happy Valentine's Day
To keep love alive is our job
To feel it, to live in it, to carry it, to share it
Valentine's Day is all that
And good creamy chocolate too

Invite Love to Invite You

Don't tell love what to do
Let love teach you what it is
Love creates the chances we take in life
Love tells us that what is meant to be will be
We have to trust to live it
Not just say we know it

We can't change most things about us
But we can grow our souls

We can recognize caring and selflessness
We can try to understand what happens around us
We can know that what we love in others
We have in ourselves

When we understand that conflict starts and ends with us
We are empowered
When we become accountable
We teach others how to be accountable
Even if it doesn't look that way at first

If we let go of needing immediate results
We grow patient in our learning
And we begin to see how things really work
That love takes time
To find, to see, to grow

When you feel impatient
Ask yourself why
Let a day pass and another
Know that the answers will come
If you are willing to wait for them

Healing is not so hard
We don't have to live with our defects
We need only be willing to see them
With a compassionate heart

If we are gentle with ourselves
We will be gentle souls in life

Others will feel our peace of mind
And your world will change because of it
It starts with love and ends with love
Love of us
Recognition of the love of others

You see we all want the same things
Be willing to know that even in the middle of a disagreement
Let love guide you
Feel your heart
It always knows what to do

The Glance of Self Love

Are you scared to love me?
Can you see that I am scared to love you?
Maybe it is because I don't know how to love me either

I have been trying to figure out how to love myself
For many years
I am still not sure what it looks like to say I love me

When I don't love myself the most
I get scared that you will not love me
When I love myself the most
I know you will love me forever

I have thought that loving myself was selfish
I thought it meant my ego was involved to do that
Then I realized that when I am happy inside
I never feel selfish
I just want to spend time with others I love

When I wake up unsure of myself
I take it out on you
Accusing you because things are not okay
When I am not happy
I don’t give you a chance to be happy with me
I blame you so I don't have to face myself

How do I love me?
I was sitting on the floor one morning
Getting ready to go to work
And across from me was a mirror
I glanced up to see myself sitting on the floor tying my shoe
I didn't see me, I saw a person tying her shoe

I realized I was a person
I stared at myself from a distance
I looked like the people I see, not the person I know

I started talking to myself
I told myself
You have a big meeting today,
I wish you well

When I said that I started to cry
It felt so good to care about me
Like the words of a dear friend
I am going to take care of you my friend
I am your friend
I see you wake up every day and rush to get ready
Yet I realized I never really see you at all

I am sorry I never looked
I judge you so harshly
And you are just doing your best
Whatever that is

I promise to do right by you
From this moment forward
I will understand when you don't think you have done well
And I also promise not to hurt you with my words
That take away from me

I also promise that when things are going great
To let you enjoy those moments for what they are
You see, acceptance of yourself is healing
That is love, love of self
Acceptance of your soul
Healing of your heart

What Is It About You Love?

What is it about you that we enjoy?
What is it about you that makes us have good days?
What is it about you that makes us smile for no reason?
What is it about us that enjoys the happiness of others?
What is it about us that feels weightlessness in love?
What is it about us that wants to hear good news?

It is our higher form
It is knowing we can
It is when we can see ourselves do something
And the path looks clear
Or clair, as in clean air

It is us when we take care of us so we have space to breathe
And take in a moment
And recognize that yes, we are happy right now
That what we have been working towards and planning for
It is here right now
And if we don't stop and recognize it now
When will we?

It is us when we feel free enough to know
Some things will never be done
And we can live with that
Other things are meant to finish and that was their purpose
We know change is why we are here
And growth is a good thing

It is us when we rest in what we know
That we don't know what we don't know
And that's okay too

It is us breathing and in our breaths
Feeling alive enough to say thank you to ourselves
For taking care of us for so long
Through all we have lived

And trust we know enough to continue
To look forward to things
And stop racing towards them

Of living now
Without the thoughts of "not now" attached to everything
It is about truth in our hearts that life is open to us
As we learn to open ourselves to what life offers

The Truth of Love Is the Love of Its Truth

We think that once we love something
It will never change
And then it does and we don't understand why

Love is fluid, it ebbs and flows
At times love is quiet
At other times love is strong and boisterous
It drives us, it carries us into situations
And we say how did we get here?

Love reminds us we are not in control
We cannot control who we are attracted to
Love makes us want to know more about our attractions

Love tells us we can do anything
Be anything, try anything, accept anyone

And if love is gone today
We always know it will come back to us
In one way or another

Some of us look for love
Others believe it will find them
Some are scared of it so they wait for it to surprise them
Others demand it and when they don't get it
They look for reasons why

Love is visual at times
Physical at times
Intellectual at times
And when it is all three
We want to stay forever

It can't be two out of three
It can't be visual and physical and stay there
It can't be intellectual and physical and be content

Because the physical will change
The visual changes
And the intellect will expand
So of course love itself will grow into another form
And we are surprised as to why or how it happens

Love fluctuates, it cannot stay the same
Because that would mean we don't grow in our lives
And we are always changing

The love of each other's truth keeps us there
We are not perfect
Expectation will make love die
Be fair in what you want from love
So that love can be fair to you

Oh Sweet Love, How Are You?

Hi love
How are you today?
You are still around as usual
I understand that if I just take a moment
I notice you

You don't come the way we think of you
So we miss you most of the time
Yet you are there even when we are not
And you wait
Until we discover you

Love, why does everyone want you?
We dressed you up
And we stripped you down
We defined you
We begged you to come to us
We think we have you one minute
And then we think you abandoned us the next

What is it about you love that keeps us looking for you?
You never change, but you change us
We rejoice when we feel you
And are thankful that you are there
When we feel sad we blame you for leaving us

Love, what do you want to teach us?

I want to teach you that love is love is love
It doesn't matter where it comes from
Sometimes you look for me in one person
What a burden you put on them!
Sometimes you discount me
When I am in a child or an older soul
Sometimes you choose who is worthy of your love

I want to teach you that you don't recognize me at times
I get left on the side of the road
And I wait for someone to notice I'm there
I'm not a person or a place or a thing
But I live in people, places, and things

I exist, but I'm not physical
I'm here and you're here
Yet you can't see me when expectation comes into play

Love is the simple happiness that tells you
You're okay the way you are
You are loved already
When you know this, you can share love with everyone

Love attracts
Love sits still and love propels
Love knows no boundaries
And discovering love is the quest of every soul
Without question

Love is a Box of Chocolates

Sometimes it's fruit filled
Sometimes it's mixed with nuts
Sometimes it is smooth and creamy
Other times it's dark and bitter

It can be milky one day
White and fatty the next
It can be filled with brittle
Or chewy and gets stuck to your teeth

It all tastes good
It is all sought after
And the variety is what keeps us coming back

Love can only be what it is
A series of flavors, colors, shapes and sizes
A box of chocolates, the mixed kind
Filled with love and surprise

Fresh and tasty
And unpredictable as to what's inside
We often pick one up not knowing what to expect
And we discover there is something to love
In each and every bite

Self Love is Not Selfish

If you do not love yourself
How can you love anyone else?
If you do not love your parents
Can you expect your children to love you?
If you do not take the time to say I love being me
Can you say I love you to another?

You see, self love isn't ego
It is from your heart
Self love is the only way to love anyone else
It always begins with you

What does self love look like?
It looks like a smile on your face when no one is around
It sounds like kind and gentle talk in your mind
You feel whole and complete when you sit alone
You smell good scents, notice colors, and taste good food

It means that you accept who you are
So that you can understand what it means to accept another
It is having compassion for yourself
When things don't work out
And feeling empathy for others when they are challenged

We cannot give what we don't have
So strive to notice the little things in your days
And watch your actions
They define who we are and why we are

Love yourself
And you will find the love of your life

Pure Love Cleans All of Us

When someone loves you without obligation
Without expectation
Without waiting for missteps

When someone loves you
Without trying to bring out your deficits
Without making you feel protective of yourself
Without you having to watch your words
Or not tell them this or that

When someone comes into your life
And you feel you've known forever
They wait for you to finish talking
They are interested in what you say
And when you need to speak about something
They listen and at the end
They tell you they know you will be okay
And thank you for coming to them
For trusting them when you need to talk

Isn't it a gift?

There are great people in your life
Sometimes that great person is you
We are the people we look for
We know enough to not take on the world alone
To share our happiness
And everything else

When we are honest about who we are
The people around us are allowed to be honest too
We draw to us who we are
We bring to us who we want to be
We have a hand in every situation of our lives

Remember every day
To be the person you would go to
And share with
And talk to
You will find the same in others around you

When we see the harshness in us
We live in the isolation of those feelings
And when we see the good in us
We get to enjoy the best of life

To believe in life is our choice
What we can be and what we have right now
We can build on it
And as we become it, it brings out the best in others

It is your job to bring the purity of love to yourself
Then everything around you will be the love you seek

Eyes of Love

When something does not make sense, it confuses energy
Hurt does not solve issues, pure intent does
To pretend in one place is to pretend everywhere
Those without remorse are the ones who blame others
For noticing what they do
Yet have you noticed that love always wins?

Love is the strongest energy of all
It withstands the test of time
Speaks from the heart
And gives without question

When love is pure we can do anything, everything, all things
The hardest part is to ask yourself if you love
Why you love, and how you love
When you know, you see it as the feeling that trusts
You remember it
When you have feelings of love, follow them, act on them
Don't tell them you will get to them when you have time

It will give you the balance to live within all things
Love doesn't have to be in everything
Just in enough things so that you can see love everywhere
Then you find love in unexpected places

If you trust love you can trust you
Look at how you live your life
Find love in the things that hurt you, it will rest your soul
Find love in the things that make you happy
And you will find more happiness
Find love in the things that make you mad
And you will solve them
When you are willing to notice you
You can see everyone else

Know that you are just living life and doing your best
When you are doing your best you will find the best of you
You have choices and part of making those choices
Is when you can see and feel the love of yourself
You see, that is the real beginning

Begin....

Love Is in the Air

Stop moving life
And allow life to happen

Control of anything narrows your path
When we can only see what we want to control
We miss all the other possibilities
Control keeps us from knowing more
Which leaves us no room to grow

Love is the opposite of control
We are here to learn, to love, to grow
Yet when we try to fit everything we do
Into what we already know
We miss the opportunities to find new ways of living

When we think of love
Most of us think of a relationship
In truth love is everywhere
It doesn't matter how love comes to you
Love is love is love!

Having a partner is sharing your life everyday
Having a child grows love to new depths
Having a parent reminds you that love is lasting
Having a friend carries love into laughter
Coworkers show you love is a team
Having a pet reminds you that love is unconditional
Nature reminds us we are part of a bigger love

Understanding the depth of love comes from knowing
That love is objective
Love is not a reason or a thing or a place
Love is a feeling
A feeling that reminds us that we are happy people
That we are caring people
That we are one of many
That we are included

And when we come across a person who loves
We understand love
And we instinctively love them

Love is the magic fuel of our lives
You cannot pump it from a tank
Pay for it
Control it
Own it
Or find it in just one place

Love is already here, everywhere
Flowing freely around you
Live in it and it will come from your soul
And spread to everything you do

You see love is not outside of you
Love is a feeling within

Love Speaks for Itself

We are so quick to say I love you
I don't know why we rush for words
When in truth it is how someone treats you
Looks at you
Comes to see you
Works with you
That tells you of love

Sometimes we look at the words
As though they are proof of some kind
Because we think we need to hear it
And then try to live up to how it is supposed to feel

What if we didn't say it?
And we just lived in love
And kept those words in for a while
Rather than thinking the other wants to hear it

Love is a feeling not a thing
Sex is truly not physical
When love is present you know it
And when it is not you feel insecure about it
Then the ego tries to prove something is there
Convincing you that the feelings will come with time

Sometimes we are so scared that we won't find love
That we settle for less before it can come to us
And then we're not sure that we did the right thing
But we figure it's better than nothing at all

If we had patience we would get to know ourselves enough
To know when we are truly attracted to another person
And to know when we are not
When it is just a momentary thing

Over time we realize we really want to be with that person
Because time told us that we care
And we can't wait to see them
And when we see them
It makes for a better day
Because love was present

You see when you feel love
Time doesn't matter
Nothing special needs to be said
No expectations
Simply that the person is there
Present, witnessing and living life with you
Side by side
No having to explain your actions
Because trust exists between you
You do what is best without being asked
And you do not feel pressure to do anything
You get to be you

Love does all of that without saying a word
I am not saying to not speak about love
I am saying that love speaks for itself

Love Takes a Stand

Forget about what you want love to do for you
And feel what love feels like
Forget about love looking like anything
And just say what you are thinking

Love is not a judge of us
Love is the open part of us
We live in the judgment and we forget
That love has nothing to do with judgment
Or conditions

Love has no on and off switch
We create requirements for it
As we try to define it
Yet love is just trying to be free like a rebellious child

Love fights us to feel it
And we tried to turn it into
A ring
A house and a car
Security
Yes, love can be all of those things if we can feel it first
And none of those things if we can't

Our souls know that love is here
And we tell ourselves it has to come from somewhere else
As though it is far away

Imagine how love feels
As we keep trying to find it in something outside of us
As it just wants to be itself
Simple, clean, clear, and available

The Smile of Love

Trust looks like
A smile
A nod
A greeting
Nothing back
Nothing forward
Just the moment that you are in

Love looks like
A deep breath
Knowledge that you are safe
A straight back
An open palm to the world

Purity looks like
A look in the eye when you are spoken to
A warm hand on your back without fear, doubt or worry
In its energy
A calm presence within yourself that says
I will do right in life without exception

Truth is all we have
Love is all we feel
And purity is what we are

Love Waits

The first rule of love is
To not forget it exists
We try so hard to find it
We overlook it when it was there all the time

The second rule of love is
To enjoy it
Love doesn't get you down
It guides you

If you noticed love
Love would tell you who you are
Then you would know
When you choose someone to love
There is always something in them that is in you
Or you couldn't see it in them

So when you meet people and you are attracted to them
Know it is the qualities you both have
That you see and love in the other person
And you can only truly love another
As much as you love yourself

So if your love of you doesn't go too deep
Don't expect a relationship to either
We expect so much from love
When we don't know what to ask of it
As though it should know for us
And then lead us to bliss

Love is as active as you are
As slow as you are
As honest as you are
Or as hidden as you are
Love is always here
Available and ready

Waiting for you to see it
And tell it what to do
Where to go
Who to share yourself with

So the next time you find yourself
Excited and happy
Don't wait for love to tell you what to do
It is waiting for you
To steer it and bring you to who you really are

Love is so simple
Yet look at how little we know of it after all this time
We wait for it to notice us
But love waits for us

The Surprise of Spring

Love has always been here
And yet it is always new
Always giving
Always receiving

Love is not things
It is remembering what was said with love
And how it felt
It is not asking anything of it
It is a warm and loving home in my heart

I am not ecstatic because of it, I am just sure
I am not high or low because of it, I am just sure
I don't know that it is perfect, I am just sure

I only want to walk and talk with you
Be there and have some time to myself too
I want to grow old here because I feel sure

Sure of what?
That there is peace between us
Trust between us
That we are friends and the love is pure

I am just happy here, where I am not shy anymore
Not thinking of what I'm doing or how I'm doing it
Like a child who doesn't yet know what is coming
It never really matters so much what is coming anymore
The moment I am in is already satisfying to my soul

Father's Days

Daddy doesn't know that we notice everything he does
His ways become ours
His thoughts are our first thoughts
His heart is open to us
Even when it closes the door to everything else
He reminds us that he cares about us
Even when he is not sure how to care for himself

Daddy doesn't know that we love him without question
We don't tell dads that we love them too often

Dad we love you
We love when you barbecue
We love when you give us a ride
Even if we expect you to do it

We missed the moments we really should have listened to you
And we thought you just didn't want us to do something

Thank you for the moments you took the time
To just let us know how things are
So that we would know
No credits, no accolades
Just love and caring
Thank you dad

You are more than a man who takes care of his family
You taught us to take care of ours
We now know to keep talking
Because kids are listening all the time
The foresight of knowing what is yet to come

Is the love of a Dad
That is second to none

Hope & Change

It's Not a Secret

How is it that if we think something, it comes true
That when we are in a great mood
Everything seems easier, lighter, freer
If we think of doing something, we just do it without effort

How is it that when you take care of yourself
You start to take care of other things too
When you clean your room
You then feel like cleaning your car, your kitchen, your dog
When you are acknowledged for doing something well
You want to do more, and do it well

How is it that you say you can't cook
Then you make a meal that tastes great
And you want to learn more about cooking
When you take a walk and notice the beauty of outdoors
You want to walk more and you feel great

How is it that when you are happy
People don't do things that offend you
And you don't take things personally

This is how we learn
That our feelings and attitudes make a difference
It's not a secret that negative begets negative
And positive begets positive

It is not a secret that truth is knowing your role in your life
And being accountable to yourself is really who you are
It's not a secret that love grows the more we feel it
It's not a secret that when your intentions are good

You feel the purity of your soul
Truth lets us live in peace
We simply need to remember truth, love and purity
And how they carry us

And remind each other when we feel frustrated
We simply forgot the truth

The secret is, it is not a secret

The Dream of Us

I went to buy some makeup the other day
I couldn't decide which color of blush was the best for me
So I asked the lady to help me

She looked up at me and I was in my sweats
My hair up in a clip
No makeup on
Just a tank top, sports bra, and shorts
And she just stared at me as she was helping me

It seemed to take her a long time
To imagine me wearing makeup
And all I could say is
Look, this is me
I dress this way every day
But at the makeup counter is the dream of me
The person I want to be when I go out sometimes
To dress in a way that makes me want to come back home
And put my hair in a clip
Take my make up off
Get back in the tank, the sports bra, the shorts

We all have the dream of me in us
We see who we could be
And we see who we are
We all want to know
That something new makes a better day
That we can go out and live life from a different angle

We think we see actors in the movies and on stage
But they are just the ones who get paid to do it
We are all the actors
And our neighborhoods are a stage
The lights are always on
We just don't see them
The camera is always rolling
We just don't notice

We are who we are everyday
And the rest is dress up time

We even dance with attitude once the heels are on
We flip our hair because it is down for a change
We eat less food that tastes better
We pay much more for things than usual

The dream of us is us too
The movie of our lives is all the days and nights
Even the ones we don't watch
Anyone can tell us who we are
Because they watch
We study each other

We see ourselves through each other
We teach each other who we are
In comedy and drama, and sometimes science fiction
Scene after scene
And as we watch
We become us

The Kid in Me Can See

When we were kids we made wishes
Now we call them dreams
When we were kids we believed in magic
Now we think it impossible
When we were kids there were long summer days
Now we don't get a chance to buy summer clothes
Before the season ends

When we were teenagers
We thought we could change the world
Now we just say that's the way it is
When we were teenagers
We knew what our problems were
And where they came from
Now the complexity of our life baffles us
When we were teenagers
We wanted to marry the first person we fell in love with
And then we learned what it meant to commit to someone

When we finished college and started working
We said we would buy a car, a house, a dog
Get married, settle down

Then we had a job, a marriage, a house, a dog, and a child
We grew new respect for what our parents did for us
How difficult some things were for them
And that they are just people too

And then we stop growing
We talk about the way things used to be
In a way that says things aren't so great now
Yet current moments are just as important as times past
And someday these days will be a pleasant memory
That we talk about with misty eyes
We forget that we get to be each age for one year
And that each year is to be cherished
For its wisdom and experience

We search for The Good Times
And miss the good moments as we walk by them

Now is the good old days
Open your eyes and see
Open your heart and feel
Open your mind and know
Open your mouth to smile

Smiling Surprise

When you are angry
Try smiling
It just may make you laugh at yourself
For taking yourself too seriously
A smile has power
To change an entire day when it is seen by another
And to change your day when it reminds you
To take yourself and life lightly

To love and forgive yourself usually comes with a smile
Smiling gives perspective
A smile affects everyone who looks at you
A smile tells the world you can handle it
A smile is the best friend of all of us
It is the enchantment of our own souls

Hope is as Hope Does

When fear replaces hope
You stand still
You feel stuck
You think you can never get out of it

When fear replaces hope
You get tired more often
You find reasons to not do things
You can't think past the fear of the moment

Yet when you have hope
You speak in solutions
Everything before you is manageable
You finish things and look for more to do

You see fear breeds fear
And hope breeds hope
Love breeds love
You feel the depth of each as they take hold

Fear is the opposite of life
Life moves and creates
Fear stops and stagnates

Hope reminds you that everything is possible
The only difference between happening and not happening
Is you deciding it will or it won't

Hope is the spring in your step
That keeps your shoes walking
And trusting that you will find what you are looking for

The Best of You is the Best of Us

When we are our best
We bring out the best of everything around us
And when we are not happy
We draw negativity to us

There is something to be said about positive thinking
Not the "everything is great" when it's not
But the knowledge that everything will find its way
That it happened the way it did for a reason
That there is something for you to learn from it
That it can be solved no matter what it is

Allowing time to teach us is important
Every question has an answer
And sometimes we may not like the answer
It is easy to accept when things work out
Yet when they don't, knowing that an answer will come
Builds our trust

We put so much pressure on ourselves
Wanting something to happen
In a certain way with certain results

Does it really matter if it does or doesn't?
How will it affect you either way?
Will it change who you are?

If you think of everything as something to grow you
It will be able to grow you
If it needs to define you
And when you are concerned about how it makes you look
It will take you on another ride completely
You see it isn't what we think we want that's important
It is knowing we are already okay

We experience things to teach us to love ourselves
Trust that when something good comes to us we deserve it
And if what comes isn't what we wanted
There is much to learn from it

We are not meant to be perfect
We are meant to learn that we can love no matter what
When we know that, love lives all around us
When we don't know that, love feels far away

Give your best to your days and your nights
You become your best when you give yourself a chance
Your best is your choice
And a way of life if you let it be

Say It's So!

If we say we can't do it, we can't
If we say there are reasons we can't, then reasons show up
If we say it will never happen, it never will
Everything is as we say it is
If we say we want, we will want
If we say we will have and believe it, we will have

Our language to ourselves is creative
We may feel humble to say "not me"
Or we make excuses saying "if it is meant to be, it will be"
But all that is meant to be will be when we do our best
When we try

Life is the adventure of trying and learning
Then coming back for more
When we are not using our minds, our bodies, our hearts
We get tired
We find fault in everything around us
Not because fault is everywhere
But because when we are disappointed in ourselves
Everything else follows

So change the language in your mind
Speak to yourself differently
Instead of thinking
That's true for other people, but not for me
Say "why not me?"

Instead of thinking
This always happens to me
Say "it happens to me because that is what I expected"
And see what happens

New ideas, different decisions, something fresh in your life
Is all already there
You just have to notice that you can say it, do it, be it

Life is for the living
If we don't try then nothing has a chance
Or we don't want it enough
Or the time isn't right
Or we really don't want to do it

Grow a filter in your mind to catch yourself
When the thoughts that take away from you creep in
When you know you are doing your best
You trust that each day ended as it should

Have trust
That if you give your best and it doesn’t happen
Then it wasn't for you
It’s that simple
It’s what it looks like to live your best

Expectation Rewind

What did you expect?
Did you want something different this time?
You can only get a different result if you try something new
Yet we to do the same things again and again
Yet we're disappointed when we get the same results

Try saying something different
When you have an opportunity to say something nice, say it
When you want to ask, what were you thinking?
Try saying, what was your intention?

If someone says something unkind to you
Tell them that you know they didn't mean it
And when you are already angry about something
Admit that everyone is a target when you feel this way
So you are better off not speaking until it passes

To not speak is a great lesson
Which gives rise to understanding
Silence is a language in itself
Silence gives you a moment to breathe
And in that moment better, wiser thoughts can be heard
Silence allows the other person to hear themselves
To sit with their words and feel how they are received

Rewind your actions and try new roads of communication
Speak a language that does not injure
Find the beauty of kindness for yourself and others
Enjoy the fruits of awareness
Love for yourself and in turn for others
The wisdom you find is that the joy of love given
Brings the joy of love received

Happy Knew Year

What is it about believing that makes it hard to believe
Why is living what we believe so hard to do
We all think we know better about many things
And then we find that we may be able to do things better
Than what we already know

Trust in yourself and your actions
In doing what you know
Think of the answers you already have
Take what you know and try it more often
Take what you feel and let it be felt
Take what you have started and finish it

We have become a society of "new" everything
We think that only new things are good things
New answers being the best answers
And we don't want anything that is old
Because we already know it

It is a new discovery to find out we already know
We find in us the answers that we already have
What is new is that we trust that we are already okay
And start from there

There are no magic answers
There is simply magic in doing
What is new is doing what you have not done yet
And letting that lead you to the new you are looking for

Bottle of Hope

What does it look like when we have hope?
We walk faster
We talk more
We involve others
We smile
We try new things
We wear different colors
We insist on trying until we succeed
We sing songs
We listen to others
It's not important that we are right

We need less sleep
We don't overeat
We exercise
And we say good morning

We listen to happy music
We dance while we are walking
We see someone having a bad day and we say we're sorry
We help someone who needs it
And we accept help when we need it

Hope is the promise of our souls
Hope is the reason we are alive
Hope is the person who reminds us
That hope is always nearby
Hope tells us that love is available
Hope is the purpose of our loving actions

Hope is the rainbow after the rain
The cool drink on a hot day
The right words when you need them
The check in the mail you didn't expect
The willingness to understand
If something doesn't work out

Hope is the reason we have an incentive to grow
To say we'll try
To change directions
To know ourselves well enough to know when to say no

Hope is not being scared when the check isn't in the mail
Hope is as alive as we are
Hope is the possibility of our hearts

Change As Usual

It is not the usual that catches our eye
It is the unusual that we remember
We don't listen when we're bored
We perk up when we hear something new
When we try something new we get excited about it
We can't wait to tell others about it
Those are the very things that excite us

Yet we fight change so that things will stay the same
When they are the same we complain about it
Life is in constant flux
Anything that stays the same stagnates like water in a pond
It sustains life, but you wouldn't want to drink it

Change reminds us that we can accept things
We can adapt and grow
We can still learn
Change takes away the fear of the unknown
And makes it known
A little change every day
Reminds us that nothing is meant to stay the same

Everything is meant to change
The possibility of change is why we research
How technology advances
How cures for disease are found
It's why we go to school

So let it apply to our emotions as well
So we can have balance
Accepting that everything changes
Changes the way we accept everything

Love's Soulvation

You can't know nice until you are nice
You can't know beautiful until you feel beautiful
You aren't happy for others until you feel happy yourself

You don't see the effort of others
Until you put forth effort yourself
You won't acknowledge another's success
Until you have felt a sense of success yourself

We cannot know how it is to starve
When we can't decide what to eat
We cannot see a heart until we can feel our own
We cannot extend a hand
Until a hand has been extended to us

When we know something then we can share it
If one of us does something
Someone else learns from it

When we see someone care
We can believe that everything has good in it
Look at your reaction to a situation
Is it to blame or be concerned that you look good in it?
Think of every circumstance as a lesson
Say thank you for showing me what that feels like
All you have to do is know the truth of any situation
And leave it for the other person to find their way

We think we need to wait for a good day to do better
We can always solve any condition
If we use our soul for a soulution

One Small Thing, Many Big Answers

We all do our best
Even when it looks like we aren't
Because then we are just on our way
To doing our best

We think of best as shiny and new
When best is really pure intent

There is a new challenge every day
Yet sometimes they carry into the next day
We go to sleep at night, but it may take a while
And wake up the next day
Often with the same challenges in our minds

What if we kept a pad and pen by the bed
And before we slept we made a list of all we think about
And wrote it all down to take it out of our minds
Then we can fall asleep
Our mind now knows of what we were thinking
And it's not just floating around worrying about the next day

Then we would wake up knowing what the day will bring
The anxiety we feel stems from thinking as we go
Yet if we settle in our minds
It is the small beginning of something big
Things that feel big become small when we write them down
It takes minutes to make a list
That clears our mind so we sleep without the racing
We start quietly trusting
That we can pave our roads
By clearing the path we walk on

Say Yes to Today

I will remember this day that I stood up for myself
And paid attention to myself
And it felt great inside to know that I can

Otherwise it becomes like all the other days
When I sleepwalk through them
Tomorrow is borrowed time
Too far away to put off feeling great in a moment

If you want to shop rather than pay a bill, pay the bill first,
You won't want to shop as much
Appreciate that you have a home, a car, a job
Rather than I have to clean my home, fix my car,
Complain about my job
Remember that these are gifts growing value in each day

Say please to yourself
Say excuse me when you bump into a wall
Walk back a few steps so you can see what you are doing
And then say thank you for noticing

Compassion will cause you to take on the love of yourself
And of everyone
Today is tomorrow
If you didn't sleep it would still be one day
You simply rested in-between

Ready, Set, Let's Lose Weight!

Whatever I said I will do tomorrow
I did today
Whatever I said didn't matter
I found out it did
And I started to do something about it

For everything I said I didn't care about
Because it hurt my feelings
I resolved within my self

What a way to lose weight
It was faster than a pound a week
Or five per month

My face already looks better
My eyes are not so serious
My laugh a little easier

It's true that we hold onto things
But it is also what is holding onto us
That holds us back from everything we want to be or do

Letting things go has to be for real
Not just saying you let go
Know that your heart wants to protect you
But it doesn't know how to resolve things
Without your free will to decide to do it

All the little things that you carry
I will do this tomorrow
This doesn't matter
I don't care that someone hurt my feelings

It all matters
It all carries weight
And those feelings are in the way of everything we do

Address these things and you will feel what you are missing
And be present in all that you do
The weight is gone when you can say
Wow, that really did bother me
What can I do today to help myself?
What can I say or who can I see or how can I change this?

Then your soul knows you are fighting for it
That you are paying attention
And that simple action
Releases many things that take residence inside of you

Losing emotional weight cleans the air you exhale
And gives your dreams a place to live again
They have been waiting their turn

So promise yourself
You will sleep physically exhausted
Rather than mentally tired
You will know the difference
And you will meet a part of you
That you have long forgotten

Would You Know You?

Who would you be if no one knew you?
What would you say about yourself?
How would you say you spend your days?
Do you love what you do for work?
What is meaningful in your life?

How flexible are you when you are challenged?
Do you know who you are with money and without it?
Are you generous?
Are you unpleasant when things don't go your way?
When you are in a disagreement
Do you think about the other person's point of view?

Do you show appreciation for the kind actions of others?
Do you remember to say thank you?
When someone observes something about you
Do you get defensive or do you consider it may be of value?
Do you speak to others as you would like to be spoken to?

These are questions of self definition
Of who you are inside and what it looks like on the outside
We are not blind to who we are
We are either willing or not to see the truth of us

Solving our problems is simply asking these questions
It reminds us of who we are
Are you dealing with your life or just passing time?
Are you growing your soul or enduring yourself?
Are you thinking before you act or are you on auto pilot?

Define yourself and you will see what you are looking for
What you are wanting in your heart
Considering why you feel unfulfilled
Trust in your ability to answer such questions
And trust the rest will come as you go along

We can't start anything
Without taking the first step
Start with the questions and your mind will do the rest
Desire truth and plant the seed
Imagine meeting you
Would you know you?

Clean Out Your Cupboards of Love

Walk away from those who let you down
Walk away from those who don't care if they hurt you
Walk away from those who set you up
From those who will talk about you if you mess up

Learn to walk away, rather than prove anyone wrong
Proving someone wrong merely drops you into a black hole
Where you join them in their ill will

You are allowed to say no
Sometimes that's how you find love and peace
You are here to enjoy yourself
Not to allow others to define you

We forget that we can say no
To what hurts our energy and takes away our peace of mind
To what reminds us of failure rather than of success
We are as successful as we want to be
We are only weak if we believe what the weak say about us

We must remember that those who talk about us
Are only doing so from their own frailty
They need to speak ill of others to feel good
They think that others cannot see them for who they are

We are responsible to take care of ourselves
By knowing that the person who challenges our wellbeing
Has nothing to do with who we are
Your challenge is to take on that energy
To realize that anyone who wants to take away from you
You need to take yourself away from

When you see ill will
Don't walk away, run
You will understand who you are when you do
They offer no benefit to your soul
You can learn from them from a distance

Love gives
When giving is not present neither is love
Through love you will always find your way
Clean out the cupboards of your heart
Throw away what is spoiled or expired

Let it go and move on
The path of self love will open a clean cupboard
Where you can store more love and freedom for your soul
Choose your Soul
And there you will find the truth of who you are
And your willingness to move forward

Is That Your Heart or Your Hurt Talking?

Is it your heart or your hurt talking?
Sometimes it is hard to know the difference
When you start thinking "I will show them..."
That is hurt
When you can turn yourself around
And know you will overcome the obstacles
That is your heart talking

Anything that isolates us
And makes us feel like we have to do everything alone
That's hurt

When we know that something simply didn't work out
That it wasn't right for us
And we get up and try again
That is our passion moving us

I watch my son growing up
And I can see when he speaks from his heart
And when he gets hurt
How he can't help but put his defenses up

I am sorry for him and yet I am not
I am happy that he knows the difference
And I see how clear he is when it is hard for him
And he will tell me
I just need to be able to feel sorry for myself
There is nothing you can say to me right now
So don't try
I just need to feel bad so that I can get this out of me
Because I don't want to carry it

He taught me that he understands enough
To know that all he needs is time to process
To absorb and then to grow

He gets hurt and then he rebounds
And because he lets himself feel things through
He doesn't carry them

Little does he know what a great gift he has
That he cleans up along the way
Rather than bury his soul's pain
Thinking he could overcome it by burying it
He understands that we can bury nothing
And if we try
We start fighting ourselves
To stop ourselves from feeling
And confronting
And then releasing
And then healing

Heart or Hurt
What if we say
Heal
The other H
When you let go
You can see
And you can breathe a deep breath that reminds you
You are whole
And it is how you handle your hurt
That gives you that breath

The Space between You and You

Believe in yourself
Without exception
Speak your truth
And don't allow judgment to follow
Wear what you love
And don't take away the joy of it

Say you can when you think you can't
Try what you think you cannot do
Experiment with new things and ideas

Go to a movie alone and buy yourself some popcorn
Treat yourself to a walk
Listen to music that you've never heard
Know that who you're talking to has something to teach you
You will find that you there is more to love
Enjoy what is new and know that you too can be new

We think we know enough in the knowledge we have now
That we know who we are and what we like
Without considering all we don't yet know

We are who we think we are
Why put limits on who that is?
We are really someone who can try things
And build on the new that feels right for us

Belief in ourselves starts with our thoughts
Our open---mindedness
Which teach us tolerance and understanding
And expands our comfort zone

We are meant to be a little uncomfortable at times
To understand what keeps us stuck
The stress of stretching moves us along

We think we know what we believe
Yet challenging our beliefs gives us trust
And allows us to see that there is always something to learn
That becomes something we love
Once you trust your beliefs
It is easier to find new things to believe in
It is the growth of your soul, one step at a time
One moment to another

How silly it is to think
That walls we create shouldn't be taken down
Let them know they are on notice
That you will be taking on the walls
And walking around them

Today is a day that you can look in the eye
And say I want to do something about the way I think

Growing doesn't come easily
But believing in yourself creates inner glow
One that stands over you and guides you
When you forget why you are trying
Believe in yourself
Leave the excuses behind

This Way or That Way

Lifetime sayings that can become life:

He did, she did, they did, anyone but I did
Poor Me stories
Everyone is doing this to me
I didn't do anything
I had a bad experience with that
No one ever told me
All I did was…
I have issues
I don't believe
It is impossible
Never
Always

Life sayings that can turn into a lifetime:

I did, I am
I will, I can
I love
It was a challenge and then I grew
I learned, I tried
I took a chance
It was not meant to be
It was meant to be
I trusted my heart and went for it
I have nothing to lose but fear
I am not scared

When something scares you, face it with a why not?
When something says you can't do something, do it
Just to know that it won't kill you

When someone hurts you, don't give it power
When someone compliments you
Say thank you and mean it

Why do we have to feel smarter than everyone else
Just to feel good?
Why can't we ask for the best for all of us
Since it will only make it better for all of us?
Why do we feel that we can't say what we think?
Why do we give someone else's opinion more weight?
Who says we have the right to expect something
When we are not willing to be something?

We can only expect what we are willing to do
We can only expect what we are willing to see
We can only expect what when are willing to say
When we do more, we learn to expect from ourselves
Rather than from others

When we speak less, we listen more clearly
When we see more, we learn to pay attention
When we are part of own lives
Our lives become a part of us

Human By Design

If you only had one of something and couldn't get another
You would take care of it
You know you could not replace it
You know they don't make them anymore
It becomes a classic, a collectable
A treasure you show all your friends
You are so happy to have such a rare find

How about thinking that you are one of a kind?
There is not another one of you
With your eyes, your teeth, your fingerprints, your voice
Your thoughts, your memories, your love
Anywhere else on Earth

You are a treasure
You are one of a kind
It is just the plain and simple truth
Like snowflakes
So perfect, with designs so subtly different
So precise
Yet from afar it looks like a bunch of snow
Yet if one falls on you
You see it for what it is
A perfect design

We all look like people
Yet within each one of us is a unique soul
We are different and the same
We have arms and legs, faces and feet, thoughts and ideas
What we do with them
Makes us a perfect design

We are perfect
And if we keep looking for everything that isn't perfect
Always on our way to being okay
We will never see the snowflakes

Perfection is love
When you feel love everything is perfect
If you don't pay attention
You will miss your unique qualities
The very ones you wonder if you have

Forgetting Something?

Don't forget that today you can smile
Don't forget that today you can eat your favorite food
Don't forget that you can solve a problem today
Don't forget that you can hug someone close to you
And no one says no to a hug
Don't forget how much it means to people
When someone speaks kindly of them

We forget the beauty of acknowledgments and high fives
Of doing what we love
So that we can love what we are doing
We forget that we don't have to settle
We do it all the time
We wait for the right moment to do something
We forget this is the right moment

It makes a difference to how we respond to each other
We are each other
Our energy is intertwined
What we do for ourselves
We have done for everyone

Our foundations strengthen
And our hearts lighten
When the load is spread in taking care of us

Don't forget that today is the day to lighten the load
Today is the day to not forget

The Flex of Flexibility

Flexibility is the bending, the stretching
The pulling and the tugging of all that feels impossible

Flexibility is willingness to endure discomfort
For the sake of learning something new
Of allowing time for the unfamiliar to become familiar
It is patience and tolerance
It is the slippery freshness of something new
It is the new pair of shoes that you have to break in

It is a challenge to embrace flexibility
When our mind is pliable
It shows us both sides to everything
Gives us happiness when we thought it couldn't be
Because we were willing to see something we couldn't see

The more you stretch your mind and heart
The easier it becomes to say you don't know something
So you can learn it
It gets easier each time you take on something new
You notice life takes less effort than before

Every big change takes a million baby steps
Each small step is a slight bend of your soul
And the flow of change becomes something you love
So your life can change into something
Better than you could imagine

Anger Smanger

What is it about anger?
When we are mad already, the smallest thing will set us off
When we are happy, nothing is a big deal

What is it about anger that clouds everything else?
Anger takes root in a closed mind
Anger does not want a solution
Anger wants to win
When anger wins there is just more anger
Coated in self-righteousness

Anger wants to blame and complain
Anger says that nothing works out
That no one cares
That it is someone else's fault

The stem of our anger is at ourselves
For not taking care of us
We want someone else to take on that job
We wait for someone else to be accountable for our lives
And blame the world for our lack of accountability

Anger becomes a familiar companion
One that we don't like but are unwilling to let go of
Most often we let it loose on someone we love
Someone so close to us, we think they will take it on

Anger is the thief that lives in a home and steals happiness
Anger is the story behind discontent
Yet we label it something else
Anger is the result of the problem we deny
The residue of hurts we hold on to
So we have to ask ourselves
What am I really mad at?
Do I want to solve it?
What can I do to take care of this and of me?
Am I telling the truth to myself or making excuses?

There is an answer we already know
If we can be clear and objective
We can find the truth
No excuses or reasons to complicate it
Just truth to heal it from the beginning
Then we get to start over

What a Spoon Can Tell You

When you walk past the sink
Are you the person who drops the spoon in
Or are you the one that walks by and cleans it?
Do you only wash it if someone else is there
Or do you leave it for someone else to clean?
Are we really getting away with anything
When we refuse to do something
Or try to get out of doing something difficult?
The truth is you either do it or you don't
Some wait until the sink is full
And others wash and dry as they go
Some can't relax until it's done

When you clean up as you go along
You clean up your mind
So you can think
And speak clearly to another
Or watch a program on TV

The spoon tells its own story
Do you hold onto your stuff?
Do you let it go?
Do you take things on
Or do you wait until everything is piled up inside
And think that someday you will clean it all up ?

Do you eat well every day
Or do you think you'll diet tomorrow and overeat today?
Are you a planner or do you let things happen to you?

Each of these are us at one time or another
Saying one thing and doing another is our biggest bluff
And blaming others for who we are is yet another fraud

Once you clean up as you go along
You are telling yourself the truth of your life

Those who choose to ignore what needs to be cleaned
Pile things up and get bogged down in the mess
They will not tell you what they actually mean
And they will only come clean when they get caught

Start washing the spoon in the sink
You will find that you finish all the little things around you
And you won't take on the weight of an incomplete life

Cleaning is everyone's job
When we choose to not carry the weight of our lives
We relieve others of carrying our burdens too
And we stop using others to do what is ours to do

Honesty isn't so far away
It is as simple as a dirty spoon
Love isn't so far away
You either share it or you don't
Truth is always around
And purity is the cleanliness of your soul
Clean the spoon, clear your mind, and move on
Clutter is not a natural part of us
Cleaning purifies and is the weightlessness of our days
And of our thoughts
Which allows us to enjoy others
Love is in the spoon

Your Soul is Not Your Body

We try to tell the world that our body is our soul
We have found ways to fill our bodies
Change our bodies
Keep our bodies from aging
Make people notice us because of our bodies

If someone is disabled we think they are less
Because they need help
If they are sick we get scared because it could be us
If they dress more fashionably than us
We think they are smarter than us

Do you really think a soul cares much about a body?
What do you believe a soul to be?
It came to earth attached to a body to teach us
Not to define us

Your soul is your heart, your intentions, your wisdom
Your body is how you get around
It's your soul's vehicle
It takes your intentions and your thoughts
And drives them into action
Your body will do anything your soul will ask of it
But your soul cannot do anything your body asks of it

When you walk away from someone
You remember how you felt
More than what they looked like or what they had
The best days we have
Are when we are not in a race to be anything

We can learn from those whose bodies cannot do for them
We see they are happy
Their secret is that they know that their soul is who they are
If we also knew that the body is part of us
Not all of us

We would understand our purpose better
When we let the truth of us show itself
We don't expect love from the outside

No one can ever walk away from an open heart
Truth is a magnet for its strength
And souls wear no masks

Close Your Eyes and See

Hope is when you can imagine something
Hype is when you can only talk about it
There is no way to start anything without starting
We start so we can get to the finish line
Yet there is no finish line
Because everything that ends starts something else

We think in terms of goals
And when we achieve them
We sometimes don't know what to do next
Goals are simply steps to greater steps

Interest chooses your goals
Goals are simply measurements
Interest is the avenue to get you there
Interests are the spark
And when the spark is lit
You no longer need goals
You gain vision
Vision is more than sight
Vision sees what is not yet here
What you can see is what you can do

Close your eyes and see
Open your eyes and do
Your paths are already here
When you can see them
You can walk them

No U Turn

We often look back in life
And remember the good parts
We romanticize them
And make them so much better than they were
We forget all the steps it took to get there
The living in between
We expect everything to live up to our skewed memories
Taking away the balance

Remember that today is like those days
You will remember the good parts in a year or two
So live better today knowing that
Our lives are not meant to live in reverse
We are meant to drive ahead and see what is in front of us
Not to take a U turn and see only what's behind us
Otherwise we would have eyes on the back of our heads
Merge onto the lanes of life
The ones that include living as you are driving
Looking around at what is beautiful today
Rather than see only the obstacles and complain about them
Complaining is easy
Park yourself in the happiness of today

Truth & Trust

Once a Door Opens, Check Out the Room

Why do we think
If we give enough to someone
They will love us
They must love us
After all, look what we have done for them

What we don't realize
Is that no one on Earth owes anyone anything
When we do things for others
And they don't react as we think they should
Know it was our ego involved and not our heart

You cannot love anyone
Any more than they love themselves
And you can't make someone love you
Or themselves
It makes perfect sense
Yet we believe our love is so strong that we can fix them
And make them love us both

You can only help someone
When they know they need help
And they want to be helped

You can love someone
And find that they don't love you in the way you define love
Unless that is their definition too
It is not that you didn't try, or they didn't try
It is our perception
And who we are on the inside
Not what we do on the outside

People are different
None better than another
We are here to learn this
So try to understand
That love has no definitions or conditions

Love because you want to
Share because you want to
Leave blame at the back door
And walk into the room
Clean it as best you can
And don't expect to be thanked

Love doesn't expect anything back
Because love doesn't need anything
Love is complete in itself

The minute you hear yourself say
If I just do this....
Ask yourself what do you need from this
And do it with your heart
Be honest with yourself
Happier about your choices
And realistic about whether it's the right place for you or not

Trust is the door that opens
Once you open one door
It leads to opening many

Midnight Intentions

If your desire is to say I love you
Say I love you
If you want something out of a situation
Say I'm doing this because...

Your intentions speak for you
You see, energy precedes words
When we don't speak what we feel
What we want
What we think
We give other reasons for doing things
And everyone feels it

People will learn that you don't say what you feel
Or what you really mean
And they know there's nothing they can do about it
So they go away
Or they don't trust you

The kindest gesture to yourself and others
Is to simply tell the truth
Then no one has to guess what you really mean
Because that is just too much work

And if someone confuses you
Simply ask them
What are your intentions?
That is something we can work with
And we can meet each other's needs

Sometimes our words are the last clue
To what we really mean

At times we think that when we say something
We can fool energy
Yet it is our energy, our intentions
That beat us to the punch

You can only feel content
When you speak honestly
You get to breathe in the relief of it
Your relationships become closer to your soul
When you trust them enough to say what's true

Don't Stop Believing

Life is so much easier when you lead with your heart
You feel good when you finish anything you start
When you smile at people they have no power over you
When they smile back, you bond in a quiet yet strong way

Life around you grows when you tell the truth and walk on
Lying never made anyone a better person
When you are happy, everything is so much more exciting
And everything that excites you finds a way of happening

Did you ever notice
That when you plan something it happens
It happens with the joy you put into the plan
Problems have only the strength that you give them
When you think in solutions problems tend to go away
You attract people to you that share your emotions
When you know what you are looking for, you find it
And when you aim at nothing you hit nothing dead center

Life is really that simple
Our trust and knowledge of ourselves
Either grows us or takes away from us
If we trusted a little more
More comes our way

Seeing is believing yet we don't see everything
Feeling is our truth telling us where we are
Challenges remind us to do something about our feelings
Creation is just you creating
Whatever we believe in enough to learn
Changes us with the learning

We know that when we are sure about anything
There is no stopping us
There really is another way
And it's not just for other people
Everything possible can belong to you

Things don't just happen
Life is so much easier when your heart guides you
Nothing is as strong as your intent
Trying anything is telling yourself you're worth it

Erase and Release

It is so much easier to hold onto things
Than to let go
It is so much easier to say we let go
Than to really experience letting go

It is especially hard to release something
If we don't know we are holding in
You have to ask yourself what you are embracing
And why you can't release it
You will find it's because you felt you were wronged
And you believe you are justified in your anger

How do we release feeling wronged?
You have to clear it with yourself first
And then with those involved
You have to admit that you feel vulnerable
That maybe you don't feel loved or cared for

And admit to yourself that you need those things
That we all require those feelings
Tell the other person
Hey, I discovered why this bothered me so much
I just didn't feel cared for
Like I didn't matter
It wasn't your fault entirely
My needs and wants got in the way
And I just wanted you to know
Thanks for listening

That alone clears the air
That alone clears your mind
It not only releases what you were holding on to
It erases it and it soon becomes a "remember when"

If you are unwilling to release
Then you are stuck with it
You need to ask yourself why you want to hang on

Does it give you a feeling of power or control?
Or maybe pride won't let you back down
Because you feel like you'll lose something
And that begs the question:
Lose what?

Speaking the truth
From your heart
It simply frees you
You can exhale
And inhale deeply
Because the truth sets you free

When We Give Up Control, We Have Control

Sometimes it seems we are doing everything right
And we expect everything right to happen because of it
And then something goes wrong and we immediately think
Why does this always happen to me?

So we try again
Thinking if we try harder we will get the right outcome
And then something goes wrong again
Why does this always happen to me?

So then we think that we have to control things more
Or they won't work out
Say the right things
Do the right things
Then it will work out the way we want it to

And we don't realize the power of control
The more control we exert the less we will do and feel
All of our energy goes into the control of what we are doing
And then ego tells us of its expectations

When we give up control we have the most control
When we have nothing to lose we have everything to gain
Because we would be happy just to learn
Instead of expecting a certain result

Desire is different than control
Desire understands the purpose of what we do
And why we do it
Desire comes from the heart

Control takes us on a path of only one outcome
And if that outcome isn't what we wanted
We miss all the other possibilities

Desire allows us to know what we are looking for
So truth can present itself and remind us
That nothing is as it seems
Or as it is seen

Desire tells us that anything is possible
When we see that there is more than one path to follow
And many ways to get there
When desire leads truth and love follow

Let It Be True!

Think of a problem you have
Any problem
A current problem
Think of what you would do to solve it
What would you do?

Would you say
Why is this happening to me?
Why is this problem in front of me?
What am I to do?

Imagine instead if you said
Maybe I had a hand in that
This is just a misunderstanding
Even though I don't agree with you

It would be more honest to think
What am I supposed to learn?
Do I want the best solution
Or do I want my solution no matter what?
How right do I need to be?

Will I feel better if I say
I am sorry we are both in this position
What can we do to solve this?

If it is someone you don't want to solve this with
Say, I'm sorry but I am not safe here
So let us both walk away knowing we don't trust each other
We are really far apart, so let us just know that and grow on
Remind yourself that we won't get along with everyone
And everyone does not have the same opinions or feelings

Think the opposite of what you would do
Run it through your mind
It will surprise you when you actually do it

You will see the response of another
Disarmed by your honesty

You see, when our egos are ruling us, we fight or we lie
It will only change a situation when we see the truth of it
And give up the fight
Then we will find a soulution

Truth is when we rest
Truth is when we see
Truth tells us what to do
Truth is when we feel open enough
To get to the love and a sense of purity

Truth is important
It is stronger than ego
Remind ego that there is always another way
It will disappear and solutions will appear!

Even a Broken Clock is Right Twice a Day

The truth of a lie
Is the lie of a truth
You cannot see something until you know what it is
We believe an untruth because we want to
And when we see the lie in what we believe to be truth
Then we know truth

Sounds like a tongue twister however it is only twisted truth
Our job, our heart's work, is to untwist the twisted truth
And speak the truth to ourselves so that we can move on

To tell ourselves that someone doesn't like us
Is only our perception
Usually on a day we don't like ourselves
When we think we can't get a certain job or a car or a house
We simply don't believe we deserve to have such things

When we tell ourselves that nothing good happens to us
We have convinced ourselves that it's just not for us
And there is nothing we can do about it

What if we thought differently?
By knowing we do what we choose to do
Then ask why we don't want to succeed
If we succeeded then we would be accountable
To live up to our goals
To have the things we want
Are we scared to fail at what we are trying for?

Even a broken clock is right twice a day
Take a chance on yourself
Start with the little things first
And then build it, one thought at a time
Take what you fear and try it
No one needs to know
Just you and your efforts

Let your efforts teach you
Have patience to teach yourself
Then share it with another
Then you will have trust

Trust in your abilities
And as your abilities grow
You become willing to try

Your love is your strongest emotion
Let it live and don't accept your own lies
The ones you have gotten so used to
That you forgot they were lies
No matter what, you will never shortchange yourself in truth

When You Are True, You Will Find You

The truth is
If you love someone and they don't love you back
They were not meant for you
And you were not meant for them

If you spend your time wanting what is not yours
You are not accepting life for what it is
You are blocking yourself from meeting the right person
And you are making yourself uncomfortable
Because inside you know the truth
The other person is uncomfortable because they can feel it
And everyone acts like it is not happening

Life tells us which way we should go
And when we don't want to see or hear or learn
We are stuck and it slows everything else around us

Energy is so much stronger than we are
Because energy is pure truth
It speaks before we speak
And we think we can change it
Because we don't want to notice what it is saying

It is like the singers on American Idol
Who say they are the best singers in the world
And the others with real talent
Who are not so sure of how good they are
They just want to sing
And they look like they would be lost or sad if they couldn't
They appreciate so much that they are being heard

Love of what you do, who you are, and what you believe in
Knowing what is yours in life and what isn't
Is the ability to listen to life
To know that life is so simple
And when it is complicated
It's because we are trying to ignore what we know

We are trained to think that if we want something
We shouldn't let anything stop us
When really if you love something in purity
Nothing will stop you
Because you need nothing back

Yet if you love someone or something
With expectations of what they will bring to you
And you think you will die without it
Listen to that sinking feeling
Telling you that it shouldn't be this hard

Truth, love, and purity are yours
If you are willing to listen to your heart
For when you are true
You find you

When the Truth Takes Over

Life is funny
In so many ways
But this way the most

Sometimes we fight the truth
Because we don't want it to be the answer
But no matter what we do
It's still the answer
Just because it's true

We ask for answers all the time
Making deals with ourselves
Saying if we just get this or that
We'd be fine
Yet our insides know better

We want to love that person
We want that job, house, car, paycheck
More money, less drama

Yet we don't move towards it
We want it and believe it isn't there for us
We think everyone gets what they want but us

The truth is you either did not define what you want
You don't really want it
Or you are not ready to get it

Ask yourself what is keeping you right where you are
You are where you are for a reason
It has very little to do with others
And very much to do with us

Nothing we can do depends on anyone else
Our enthusiasm and love and passion drive us
If we suppress any part of us we can't move forward

The truth of us is in us already
When results are not as important as doing what we love
Then our ego is not present
And we can move forward

It's not about finding out who we are
We are right here, in front of ourselves
Screaming, can't you see me?
Just take a look, speak the truth
Tell yourself how you feel and grow on

Don't lead with thoughts of discontent
Put the good stuff first, it will never let you down
Trust in the truth is all the truth needs

Don't Take This Lying Down

Why do we lie?
We lie to make ourselves feel better
To convince others we are something we're not
To hide things we don't like about us
To try to cover up our insecurities

Sometimes we lie to get something from someone
Or to take something that isn't ours
To try to change a situation to our advantage
Or simply because we don't trust life enough to tell the truth

The bottom line is that a lie cannot do better than what it is
A lie is a lie is a lie
Any lie we tell is a lie to ourselves
When we lie to ourselves
We are saying that we cannot handle our own truth

We try to convince ourselves that a lie doesn't matter
So that we can manipulate life
Yet life is truth, and cannot be manipulated
For truth is stronger than any lie

When we lie we throw away the meaning
Of everything we do
Because we know we lied
We cheated ourselves and everyone around us

Telling a lie says that you are not worth the truth
So when we hear we are deserving of good things
We discount it because we know better
We know we lie

A lie never hurt anyone more than the person telling it
Lies don't give, they only take away
And the liar blames others for not noticing that they lied
So they don't respect those they lie to

When you are speaking to someone, ask yourself
Are you telling the truth?
If you are not, then stop talking
You are wasting your time and theirs
And if you are telling the truth
You will walk away with something of value
Your integrity

Lying is easy, it takes no effort
When a lie is told, both parties walk away with nothing

Tell yourself the truth and your mind will stop racing at night
Tell yourself the truth and you will stand tall with grace
Tell yourself the truth and you will not worry about reactions
The truth is the truth
Speak the truth and all will know it's the truth
The energy of truth carries everything forward

The Lie and the Truth

Lie: Hello Truth, tell me about yourself
I am the Lie
I am the opposite of you

Truth: I am here all the time
And sometimes no one can see me
I stand out in a crowd and people walk around me
I am present at every meeting
And no one talks about me
I am in every conversation
Yet not mentioned at times
I feel unloved and do not get much attention at all
At times I am jealous of you lie
People get excited when they talk about you
At least for a moment

Lie: Yes, but it makes them feel bad and then they don't like me so much

Truth: But at least you get honorable mention in political events

Lie: Yes, but then they write about me in the papers the next day and they question me

Truth: Oh...And then what?

Lie: Then the person who is found out gets in trouble
And then they say they want nothing to do with me
They say they hate me because I make them hate themselves

Truth: Hate?

Lie: Yes, I have to use that word, I hear it all the time

Truth: Well, I guess not being talked about isn't so bad
At least when they find out about me it solves things

Lie: Yes, and you get to say who you are Truth
When they find out about me, they deny they ever knew me
They try to make up excuses and they throw me to the wind

Truth: Oh...I have nothing left to say...
The truth is, you can't change me,
I am what I am, and I never really change
All I wanted was some recognition,
now I feel like I don't need it so much
I am already happy,
I guess I just wanted to be remembered

Lie: Oh, Truth, they will remember you, they have to
Otherwise no one would sleep or enjoy their meals
No one would have friendships or partners of any kind
A child wouldn't have anyone to talk to without you
Truth you serve a purpose
When people find out about you, they can't live without you
Being a lie is just a lie
I am not really here, I just think I am
I am not real and nothing about me feels good
You are stronger than me, you last longer than me
Thank you Truth, now I can rest
I will try not to let others use me so much
I think it is your turn now to undo the troubles that I made
I think I can change my ways
I want to be like you
I love you Truth

The Stem of Trust

Many mishaps come from lack of understanding
Of what trust looks like, rather than what it feels like
We see better with our ears than our eyes
When we hear someone speak
We see the person who speaks as well

Do we trust what we hear?
Are we wanting to see differently?
When people do not trust us
Is it because we don't trust ourselves?

To be trustworthy
Is to trust in ourselves
When we act in truth, it can be felt by all
Everything really is as it seems
When we can see clearly
And when we are not ready for the truth of a situation
We only see it as we think is should be
And misunderstanding happens

Trust in your instincts
They exist for a reason
We always know when we do something that is not right
We have to learn to ask ourselves why we did it

We all have a defining moment
When we take a road that isn't right for us
And we just keep going trying to prove it is right
We ignore what we feel and know
We fear accountability
We judge ourselves and think we can't simply turn around

Do it anyway and grow your belief in yourself
Do it and trust that you can
Do it and give yourself the satisfaction

That your instincts serve your truth
And truth gives you vision
And vision leads your heart
To a life that you ask for and are too scared to know

The stem of love can only grow if you plant the seeds
The seeds are your love, truth, and purity
They are the pyramid of your thoughts
And action grows your trust
You know what trust looks like, feels like, and is

The Truth

When truth comes to us it cannot be controlled
And sometimes we get angry at the truth
But truth is not harsh
The real issue with truth is that it cannot be changed

We are used to changing things that we think we don't like
But the truth does not give us wiggle room at all
It just is

Truth gives to us an avenue, a path, a bridge to itself
It cannot pretend something isn't happening
Nor can it tell you what you want to hear
All it can do is be itself

When truth speaks to us
And we don't want to hear it, we say
Please go away, I have found a way to get around you

And we spin until we get dizzy
And finally we give up
For our soul is always searching for the truth
And it won't give up until we see it

When fear and doubt and worry
Find out how small they really are
And truth takes center stage in blaring lights
Only then we can see the show

Let truth live
For love is right behind it
And we can only find love in the light of truth

Healing Love

When you can say
I didn't mess up, I thought I was doing my best
There are no mistakes, this happened for a reason
What am I supposed to learn from this?
I acted that way because I was feeling insecure
Why did I feel insecure about that?

The truth will heal your soul

To have compassion for yourself
Is to heal your soul
When you listen to what others say
And it becomes louder than your voice
You feel compromised, because you are

Listen to your own voice
And understand your intentions
Know the whys of your actions
Then there can only be understanding for yourself

Self love is when you change the actions
That are not your best
And understand you are simply growing
Into who you see yourself becoming
To know you can't change anything that happened before

And to know what you can do
You can live in this moment
You can decide what you want to do today

As your trust grows, you grow
As you grow, everything else grows around you

The Depths of Love

At times accepting love is the hardest of challenges
We have had times in our lives
When we were hurt or someone let us down
When we let someone know how we feel
And they said something unkind

We start censoring ourselves
We say "I won't do this again"
"I won't trust anyone with my heart"
And we think of others in this way

We think other's intentions toward us are not good
And we become defensive
We hide our true feelings
And we are on guard
Only when we are alone, we feel safe
And yet we don't want to be alone

This thinking becomes a way of life
In time we start to proclaim that we are protecting ourselves
And in the process we conceal our most precious feelings
We feel alone with the best of who we are

Then we meet someone
Who isn't hiding, who isn't holding back
Who isn't covering up who they are
We are immediately attracted to them
Because nothing is more attractive than trust
They remind us of who we could be

We want to know them and we want to be that person again
We wonder what happened, how we became this way
A shadow of ourselves
What do we really think?
What are we really feeling?
How is it to be open in that way?

Love is common to all of us
We all have it, feel it, and long to share it
Yet when we are growing up
And love is scarce, we grow fear
As though that's the way it should be

We find out that is not who we want to be
When we see someone who is free in love
We remember we want to feel it more
Yet we think we are an exception to love

When someone loves us, we don't believe them
Because we have stopped feeling love for ourselves
And we have become accustomed to living without it
We are not so sure how to live with it
Sometimes we even try to hurt the person who loves us
So we can avoid feeling it

This is where accountability comes in
A soul has to account for why it is running away from love
And know we lost the love of self somewhere along the way

Speak to yourself, in your heart
That you are a person who wants to feel love, to be love
That you are not an exception

Let yourself feel it, and don't try to push it away
You have to breathe it into you, all the way in
Love is already here
It already exists

The reason we are here is to find it
We all feel lost because we aren't doing our job
The job of understanding that we are part of each other
Of knowing we are all here to love

Once love is known
It never ever goes away, we will never lose it

Even if we forget for a time
We know it's there because we felt it

Love grows you and it understands its strength
Love is loving enough to wait until we find it

Hearts of Innocence

One night as my son was getting ready to sleep
He said to me
"Mom do you think He has something good in store for me?"
I said, "Who?"
He said, "God?"

I told him yes, and then I thought
About how I don't talk about God to him very much
I didn't know his feelings about God
And he showed me he is living with God
Knowing there is something more, wondering about his life

I remembered it for days
And now I'm writing about it
We all want to believe there is more to life than we see
And in that bigger life we are going to be fine

The innocence of our souls
Gives us the reasons to try and to try again
Loving what we know and finding new loves
To live in the truth of our innocence

Innocence is such a far away word at times
When we say someone is innocent
It implies they know less than us
Yet innocence is truth spoken
And truth is wisdom
When truth is spoken our hearts are talking
And that is how we touch each other
And when we touch each other
Is when we are most alive

Don't Be True to Me, Be True to You

You tell me about yourself by what you do
If you ask me not to tell a secret
You ask that of others too

If I see you lie to another person
You most likely lie to me too

If you wash your hands before you eat
I know you wash everything else too

If you are willing to take something that isn't yours
You will steal from me too

If you talk about others
Then you talk about me too

It isn't what you confide in me
Confidences need not be
If it is worth saying it must be true
And if it's true it's not a secret

You are not any different in front of me than behind me
People are the same in all places
We cannot be one way here and another way there
How you treat others is how you treat everyone

We ask many things of each other
The most important is to ask for the truth
So that we can trust each other to act with respect
Then we know we are always respectful

To clean up after ourselves
So that we can clean up after each other
Which leaves us feeling clear
So we know our intentions are clear

We learn a lot from each other
By watching and noticing
And we react from that truth we see

Your children don't hear you as loudly as they see you
Your friends see you for what you have done
Not for what you say you have done
And your heart knows the truth no matter what you say

Truth is here and it waits for us to see it
And then to be it
We say we are looking for it, yet we already know of it

Once you are true to you, you can be true to me
Once you start speaking with your heart
Others want to be in your heart
When you act with clean hands
You speak with a clean mind

Wash your life with truth and let truth create the path
There are not many paths, truth is the only path
Anything else leaves as fast as it came
But truth stays with us forever

Truth is the breath of our souls
And the soul of your breaths
You can share your heart when you feel its purity
Your purity is your most attractive quality

Life with Momentum

You know when you start to live in the moment
It is when you stop complaining and feeling nervous
Or wanting to take things out on others

You know when you start to live in your dreams
It is when you love what you do
And work is not a burden, it is who you are

You know when anything is possible
It is when "no" is not an answer

You know when you have arrived
It is when you see the world without fear, doubt, or worry
Of how the world sees you

Fear & Ego

Affording the Cost of Love When Ego Comes So Cheap

It is easier to love than to feel bad
Yet we feel bad more than we love
We all have baggage of some sort
Is it meant to stir us up and get us going
Or stop us from living our best life that we can?

There are two kinds of people
Those who use their baggage to get what they want
And those that use it to avoid getting what they say they want

Our ego wants, love simply gives
Ego tells us things that say we are not loved
Not worth it
Don't deserve it

Love says you can do it, I am here and I will stand by you
Ego never provides what is needed
While love gives all that we need

We live in a world
Where we think that ego is the way to be
We think if we get what we want then we will be okay
Yet when we get what we want
Ego replaces it with another want

Love is so simple it is overlooked and forgotten
Because we don't believe it is there
It doesn't talk to us as loud as ego does
It doesn't boss us around
It doesn't take anything away from us

When love talks to us we discount it
Because we cannot afford to feel it
It would open us up too much
And it is much easier to fight than understand

Every day we think of these things
I don't want to do this or that anymore
I want to get more
I want to accomplish

Ego is so tricky
It wants to test you and push you, and it wants to win
Yet there is nothing to win at the end of the day
Love is the lasting trust that you grow in yourself
Love is the way you have patience to know
Everything will find its way
All you have to do is do your best

Ego tells you there is always something better
Than what you are doing
Love says you are great already

What do you want to contribute to the world you live in?
Love is the springboard
Ego is the diving board without a pool

Ego is abundant
You can find it on any store's shelf and it's cheap
Love doesn't have a price
It is as priceless as your favorite person
Your children
Work you love

Love is the glue that attaches to you forever
And when you find it
You get attached to it too

Hearty Living

Fear, doubt, and worry will only stagnate you
The only thing between can't and can is you
Your mind is powerful enough to stop you
It can also be powerful enough to start you

Maybe we got the power of the mind thing all wrong
Thinking our mind will do anything we set it to
However we forget to include our hearts in the decision
We forget that our hearts can tell our minds what to do

Our hearts balance our minds
Our minds can easily think of ego
About who or what is better
Setting our goals only to show someone something

Really your decisions show you who you are
It doesn't matter what anyone else thinks
If you don't think it yourself

You see, others see you even though you think they can't
Just like you can see what others don't want to show you

Show yourself as a person you love
And you will grow yourself into someone to love
Someone who can stand in their own integrity
We remember those who stand in their convictions
And we learn from them without words

Tomorrow no longer is far away
And today is yours to live in
So live

Integrity Is a Force to Reckon With

When someone is verbally assaulted
And they have integrity
They don't need to fight back
When someone is angry
And they thrust their anger at another
Integrity knows it isn't about the person receiving it
It's about the attacker

When someone is not happy
They do not want you to be happy
When someone is happy
Then everyone else is okay

You see, people's behavior is not special to you
They are the same everywhere
Just like you are the same wherever you are
If we can walk away when another is on the attack
We just taught them something
We taught them that we are just a mirror
Not the problem

We are going to have days when we are the attacker
And others we are the attacked
All we need to know is the why we are either
Our integrity will tell us and we can choose
To make it worse or make it better
Do I fight an angry person?
Or why am I so angry I need to let it out?

Integrity knows the difference
Knowing the difference heals us
And the path of growth can pave itself

How Could You

How could you not do what you want to do
How could you not say something you want to say
How could you constantly procrastinate
How could you not like who you are
How could you come to the end of your life and say
"I always wanted to do that but never did…"
"I always loved him, her but never said so…"
"I always wanted to go to…I never tried…I hoped I would…"

How could we live life and not do what we desire
As though someone told us we couldn't
We are the only one stopping us
We are the only one who can say no

In life we think of so many reasons why we can't or shouldn't
Or that we are stopped by things outside of our control
Yet none of that is true
It all comes down to love

If you truly love something, express it
By expressing it you are making it real
By making it real you are making it possible
By making it possible you are one step closer to it
By allowing yourself to think of it, you are excited about it
By allowing yourself to talk about it
You are knocking down your own walls
So you can keep walking toward it

Let the good in, whatever your good is
Let your wants seep in without guilt
Replace guilt with love
Love is understanding and compassionate

When you are happy, those around you are happier
When you are happy you have much more to give and share
When you are happy you say yes

Do what makes you happy
Take a day off to hear yourself think
Eat well and you will feel better at the end of the day
Remember how far you have come for a moment
Go to an ocean, mountains, open land and gain perspective

Remember the moments of your life that changed you
Remember that no matter what you have been through
You always come out okay
In fact better and wiser than you were before

How could you not do what you love?
If you ask, you will find you can't

Life's Nectar

Watch your steps
Walk in peace
Listen to the heights of your mind
And react with time in your thoughts

In your moments of relaxation
Take walks
The walking is the peace of your mind
It is an energy in itself
Which takes you to the roads of understanding love

The idea of self love has been manipulated by the mind
Making us believe ego's version of self love
That thinking of ourselves excludes others
Instead of giving true love to ourselves
So we can love others

So simple is the truth
So complicated is the mind when it realigns truths
To accommodate ego
Truth settles and all the rest leaves us with questions

True self love understands the value of love itself
Love given freely to ourselves and to others
You cannot offer anything you do not possess within

Fear of love does not have a place
Fear is the driver of a car with no engine
You simply cannot drive the car

There is nothing to lose in love
Freedom to speak from your heart
Love enough to say you have learned
Compassion to care for yourself
The heart calms when you know you are present

Then you can share you
Give what you have
And receive what is given

Ego's Friendly Fire

We hear about the bombings
Of Iraq, of Palestine, of Afghanistan
We think to ourselves, it's okay because they are terrorists
We see the devastation and we say
It's okay, they kill people for their religion

We see mothers cry and we think they are different mothers
Brothers in search of survival
Sisters in search of a future
Grandparents unable to protect
Parents unable to make a living

Education is scarce and interrupted
And it is all okay because they are Arabs
Because they are Muslims
Because they do not deserve
What everyone else in the world deserves
Not protection
Not food
Not entertainment
Not even water in some areas

They should be lucky we call them people
For in our hearts we equate them to animals
Yet we do not dare to speak it in words
Instead we say it in actions

The Palestinians were simply living on the wrong land
What they have become is a result of that
The Iraqis happen to live on an oil rich land
We all know if Iraq traded kumquats
They would still have their country
Afghanistan is included because they grow terrorists
Iran is a threat because they may advance in knowledge
Yet other countries do so unabated
And we all stand by and take away their humanness
Simply so we can sleep at night believing they deserve it

We starve ourselves as we starve others
We hurt ourselves as we hurt others
We pretend that is not truth either
We simply want to believe we are better than others
We want to use others to justify our actions

Our leaders reach out for money
The money it takes to kill others and control them
Could repair our world's ecology, economy, and love
We got to a place that says we won't do that
We want love on our terms, not God's
We let ego run the world
Greed motivate our decisions
And we are crumbling beneath our own weight

We are finding power in our hands is not a good thing
We steal with it and we fear losing it
To believe that self motivation produces anything good
Is the perception that we are better than others
Because we think we can control everyone

Eternal paths bring growth to all souls
As God Almighty says we are one
We say we believe in God, in forgiveness, in truth, in trust
Yet we do not understand the meaning of love yet
Love is love is love
To think it is a game of elimination is to eliminate all of us

The Invisible Wall

Take on your worst fear
Identify it
Are you scared to tell someone you love them?
Do you think you will not be loved back?
Do you not know how to say what is bothering you?
Are you ignoring something that doesn't feel right?
Are you scared to change careers?
Do you fear that your dreams are not going to happen?
Do you not want to admit that a relationship is not working?

Whatever it is, write it down
Put it in an envelope
You may never need to look at it again
You have given your brain a path
To the other side of your fear
You have taken something you thought was big
And made it small

A thought process that will teach you that fear is only fear
Fear only has the strength you give it
We can do what we fear
When we see it is the fear that holds us back
Not the very thing we fear

When we put it in perspective by having the courage to see
We see the other side of fear
And it is nothing
Fear is blinding
When we see it for what it is
We find that fear is a small thing without a foundation

Fear is invisible, yet we can build a wall with it
And believe it is real
Yet the wall can be walked around
Anywhere, anytime, whenever you decide

When you can see how to settle in one area
You can invite others in
And they too will learn the other side of fear
Teach by doing

It is a decision with a return on the investment
Your life with benefits
As many as you can accept

Why is Insecurity so Popular?

Why is it when someone says something nice about us
We take it away with our mouths
We say it isn't true, or it isn't much
Yet we want to believe it so badly

Why is it when someone says something that hurts us
We believe it
And we think unkindly of ourselves
As we replay those words over and over

Why is it that love has a hard time being seen
When we don't feel good
Why is it a challenge to take in praise or thanks
Yet if no one praised or thanked us we would point it out
First to ourselves and then to others

Why is it that someone has to be bad
For us to be good
Or that someone has to fail
For us to win
Or someone has to be less
For us to be more

When we are unhappy about ourselves
We think of these things
When we are not sure ourselves
When we feel like we need to prove ourselves worthy
We don't feel the love of us
So we believe that others are not capable of loving us

When a conversation involves tearing down another soul
Ask the person why they noticed that
When we are all just doing our best

The saying "you spot it, you got it"
Is more truth than we can handle at times
If we find ourselves digging into others

We should immediately ask ourselves
Why do I need to do this?
What is missing in me
That makes me focus on another's shortcomings?
What is it that I am not ready to solve, to see, to be, in me?

When a person comes to you with ill will
You can walk away rather than stay and engage
You will know who you are if you do
And what you are looking for from life
That life does not happen to you
You happen to life

It is all about choices
What we choose to say
And not say
How we interact
What we do
And choose to be a part of

Pay attention to you
You are your partner
You can be who you want to be
Anywhere you decide to take you

Break Bread, Burst Energy

Know that if others are not happy
Our chances of being happy are less
If we hurt someone
We are waiting for someone to hurt us
If we think evil exists
It does simply because we are looking for it

So when you run across a person
Who is broken inside
Instead of breaking them more by adding to their anger
Say "Hey, what's up?"
And they may say something mean
And we may want to respond in kind

Stop yourself
And say, "Hey, I know you didn't mean that"
"Let's try this again"

It may sound silly to do that
But a person only acts that way
Because they were never heard or noticed
And they feel like no one "gets" them
And they have an automatic defense in place

Breaking the energy of anger and self doubt
With a simple "hey" from the heart
Lets them know that you just want to be there
Without a reason or explanation

It gives them a break to know that you're there
Without judgment
And they can breathe the air you breathe

You see, we can't be happy alone
We need each other to be happy together
Our happiness depends on all of us
That is why we fight so hard for the "we" of us

Deep down we know
That we are not meant to be alone
And happiness waits for us to catch up
For everyone on Earth has the ability to laugh
And smile
And to remember the best of us
When we allow the us of us
To be the we of us

Run Don't Walk Away

We don't like to not like someone
It takes a lot for us to say we don't like someone
We try to give them the benefit of the doubt
We give chances, and we say they are not that bad

Yet there are some people who will come into your life
And no matter what you do or how much you help them
They find a way to say the worst things about you
You cannot believe a person could say such things

They will gossip about you
And let others form an opinion based on falsehoods
And somehow they feel good about it
As though they accomplished something
They justify what they say by creating stories
They find power in getting others to join in
They don't feel so bad if they can get another to believe it

And you feel the energy of it
You can't fight it, it has already grown a life of its own
Because ill intentions keep it going

It is better to be the one talked about than the one talking
The one talked about is doing and living
The one talking is covering up for what they are not doing
They try to keep things as down as they feel

When you hear someone talk about you
Or about someone else
Walk away and know that time will answer every question
It is easy to talk about anyone

The higher road is the road of love
Love enough to trust
That you are one who would not do such things
And others will know that about you too
That you are a person of trust

Love is open
Truth is clear
And when the air is murky
Run don’t walk away
And don't look back
The talkers are stuck back there

Fear or Flowers

Fear gives us reasons to not do something
The reasons to not try
The reasons to say we can't

Fear gives us reasons to turn logic into the illogical
To say I have issues with...
To say I don't deserve to have this person, job, or thing
To say I didn't because...

Fear will make us do things we don't understand
Say things we don't mean
Attach to people for the wrong reasons
Make choices that are not good for us
Fear wants to take control
It says to us, I am taking a little bit of your life every day

We forget that we can talk back to fear
We can tell fear it is not our friend
We can tell fear it can no longer play in our playground
We are going to remove the equipment
And plant seeds
We are going to plant flowers of color and purpose
And water them

We will listen to music as we pull the weeds
We will tell the garden it can grow now
Without all of the heavy equipment on top of it
The rusted metal and bent slides are gone
Every time we want to use fear to stop us in life
We will go to the garden and see how life grows
How simple it is to grow beautiful flowers
Without the clouds of fear overhead

Fear is there when we need an excuse
To not do something we want to do
And then one day we won't need the excuse
And the flowers will continue to grow

For the sum of us is the growth of our souls
And the soul of us is the sum of our growth

Imagine Life without Ego

Imagine if there was no ego
No me, me, me
No I have to have this or that
No I want I need
No if only I had

Imagine if you didn't think you needed a better house
A better car or job
Imagine if you didn't believe those things mattered

Imagine if you never had to lie
Embellish a story
Avoid accountability

Imagine if you didn't need attention
To feel better about you
You didn't need compliments about how you look
To feel acceptable
Or you didn't buy clothes to look like someone else

Imagine if you didn't have the pressures of ego
That voice that pushes you in the wrong direction
And then leaves you feeling alone
Imagine not having to feel like others don't love you
Or want you around

Imagine if you recognized ego's weakness
Instead of believing what it tells you without question
Imagine no restrictions on what you think you can do
Ego really has nothing to offer
The love of your soul offers the truth of you
Yet it seems weaker because it is a quiet knowing

A soul's strength is in its silence
A soul lets you come to it
Waits for you to find it
Knows the lessons of your days will bring you to it

Your soul's language is silence and love
Caring and compassion
No race to a finish line because it is forever

Your soul is loyalty
The part that knows better and tugs at you to do better
It reminds you to see your role in everything

Your soul is your partner and a warrior
That battles your ego everyday
That pushes you to find your passion
And live it

Your soul is the strength of your convictions
The kindness in conversation
The love that you share

Your ego sets you up to compete
In games where there is never a winner
Ego tells you people are against you
That the work you do is not enough
That you should doubt the choices you make

That you should worry and fear
That you didn't take the right road
Or make the right decisions

Your soul is your keeper
Keeps you close to who you are
With compassion for yourself

Your soul is as calm as you strive to be
It does not judge
It needs nothing from you

Its only demand is for you to remember to love
Since that is all it is

It commands your honor
And teaches you dignity
Your soul is your heart
It beats in your mind
And waits for you to hear it

Everything for a Reason

When you don't feel included
It makes it easier to justify hurt feelings
You think you want to do everything yourself
You build resentments and you don't want to include others
When you don't feel included
You learn to take care of yourself
And try to not care that you aren't included

Yet it all starts in learning to include yourself in your life
Make time for yourself so that you have balance
For time with yourself and with others
The time with yourself will open doors to others
For what you have in common
You will find others that have the same desires as you do

Nothing is as it seems
Everything really does happen for a reason
And every time you are not included in one place
It simply means you belong somewhere else
If you are not with a certain person or at a certain job
It means it wasn't yours yet or maybe never will be

The time to yourself
Teaches you acceptance and patience
Acceptance of the people and things that come into your life
And of those left out of it

In truth, it is not that you are not included
It is simply your freedom to find where you are included

Ego Talk is so Dated!

When someone's ego is talking
We can't hear them
We don't want to hear them
We have nothing in common with them
And we quickly forget them
Like vapor in the air
They were never really there

When we run into ego in us
We remember all the stuff we don't like about life
Then why do we listen to it?
Why do we act foolish when we want love the most?

We try to act like we don't need to love anyone
So we toot our own horn when we feel the worst
When we don't know how to ask for love
We try to convince others we are doing great
Better than others
We think if they believe it they will love us

Yet people will not be convinced
They will walk away and wonder what just happened
Then they avoid us because they feel uncomfortable

Listening to boasting or putting someone down
Makes us all nervous
We know that we could be the next target
And we wish we weren't there to hear it

What do we do when we feel unloved
And our egos start taking over?

It's usually a good time for a time out
To lay low and let ourselves feel what is really going on
So that we can see us
And then others can handle seeing us

You see, it isn't what others think that drives us
It's just what covers us up
Once we have put on the show we too feel bad
And we don't want to be around ourselves

When we can say to ourselves
This is what I feel like and look like when I'm feeling down
It just means I need to be quiet for a while
And hear myself clearly

We need time to rejuvenate when we're running on empty
We can't expect that every day will be as we'd like it to be
It all boils down to knowing our intentions
And when our intentions are clear so is everything else

When we have a real conversation with ourselves
We can have real conversations everywhere else
And we will be felt
And we will be heard
And we will know
That to be loved is not to make people love us
It is to love ourselves enough
So we can love others
So they can love us

Fear is Ego's Biggest Sword!

When our focus is on fear
Fear has no choice but to happen
And then fear rules

We try to stop things we fear from happening
So that we won't have to face them
Then we won't have to be challenged

We spend our lives
Trying to make things not happen rather than happen
Trying to prevent something we fear
Instead of focusing on what we love

It's a shift in our thinking
To take us from thoughts of fear and failure
To growth and acceptance of anything that comes our way
When we think anything can happen
Anything is allowed to happen
And when we only focus on what we fear
Lo and behold fear happens
Then we say "I knew this would happen!"

When you fear something
Ask yourself why you fear an outcome
Why are your expectations powerful?
What do you need to avoid and why

Fear is ego's best tool
Fear is the greatest obstacle of our time
Fear is the sheep dressed in wolf's clothing
For fear only has the power we give it

Fear is the reason we resent ourselves at times
Because we let it tell us what to do
And how to live
And we don't question it

What in life do we do without question?
When we buy a car, we search the Internet, we call friends
We shop around
We buy a house the same way
We try on several pairs of jeans before buying
Yet when we feel fear we don’t question it
We simply accept it

Say no to fear and your heart will thank you
Your soul will get to contribute to your decisions
And your free will can be heard

Fear, who are you and what do you want from me?
I know I can live without you
I came to Earth without you
And I was just fine until I met you
You are a relationship I don't want to keep
I can see you for what you are, an obstacle and a trap
I think I am better off without both of those

Fear, you are an empty word to me now
So go away
I need the space you so unexpectedly filled
Once you’re gone I see the places I have for other things
Wow, this big empty room
To be filled with who I am without you
And I am not even scared
Because you are not in me anymore

Ego Dresses as the Prize

Why are we surprised when ego rules us?
It sneaks in when we aren't looking
And sinks its teeth into our minds
Ego lies to us and when we believe it
It gets to continue on its path
Until the truth shows up

The ego doesn't recognize anything beautiful
Because it is too blind to see
Too stubborn to wait
Too ignorant to know there are other possibilities
It creates expectations that cannot be met
Doesn't account for others
And pretends it didn't do anything when things go wrong

Ego needs only to get your attention
And when you give it an audience it takes over
Then it will convince you
That the feelings of desertion, loneliness, failure, frustration
Are because of you, not ego

Ego tells you that you are less than others
And better at the same time
Ego is hard at work
Until the truth of your soul peeks through
And tries to fight it
And that is your conscience
Ego is the friendless friend, the mindless mind
The blind eye, the empty heart

Ego is not even the friend of itself
So why is it here?

If ego could speak honestly to us, it would say:
I am only here to challenge you
Your job is to recognize me enough to make me go away
I am the opposite of love

I will teach you to find love in spite of me
If you tell the truth, I cannot exist in you
Until you do that, I am here to stay
I am the catalyst, the opposite of who you really are
I don't think of you, care about you, or want to help you
I am very good at hiding; you don't even think I'm there
You think your thoughts of lack and limitation are yours
But that is really me
And I am a master of convincing you of those lies
It is your job to be stronger than me
And until you are, you are my playground

Your soul can say:
Ego, you are an old thought
And you have made yourself a habit
I can see you creep up on me
And make me worry, blame, deny, and lie
I will know it's you and I will push you away
I will remind you that you're not welcome here
You see ego; you are really vapor
You leave with a simple sigh of truth from me
Truth is stronger than you
And I can only say it with love, another of your enemies
It is an ongoing battle, but I know what to listen for
When you think you have a chance
I will remind myself that I don't have to allow you in
I am stronger than you
Once I see you, you will know
I will be the one asking you to leave

Ego Becomes Egone

When fear stands back
Passion steps in
Some passions have waited a long time
To step up
Passion is the bubble that seems to burst
Each time something gets in its way

There is so much we want to do
And when we can't get to it
We feel nervous energy in and around us
We feel we are not enough, we let ourselves down
Or that we have unfinished business in life

We race, yet we never finish
We rush, but we never rest
It has become a state of mind, a way of life
We want everything without thinking why

It is the gas pump of life
Will we fill up on ego, love, or truth for the day?
Ego is the most expensive
Love is free; you just have to ask for it
Truth is also free; you only have to speak it

We seem to choose ego until we have time to ask
Why we are making such a choice
When we don't ask
A day goes by, a week, month, a year and sometimes years
We start to feel we don't know ourselves
Like we are far away from our hearts

When we find ourselves battling ego
We use words like I want, I don't have, I never get
No one understands, less than, better than
It is really hard to fight internal greed
With truth pushed aside we can't see the path
To what we really want

The opposite of ego is truth
Ego dissipates when you don't lie to yourself
When you do not speak ill to your soul

When you think of problems as challenges
When you see that you create all that happens in your life
When you account for your role in your life
When you ask yourself "why am I letting ego take over?"
Then you find your way to truth and love

The real questions arise
When you ask why you can't see what you have
Why you only see what you don't have
The days of deficits are gone
It's time to rebuild our minds

Start in your heart and start today
Tell yourself you will speak the truth to yourself
And find out how liberating it feels
Just do your best
And know not everything has to do with you alone

If each of us does our best, our world is its best
When we are all racing the world feels like it is racing
When we rest the world feels like it rests
We can live in truth and love
And ego can become egone

Fear of Love is Love of Fear

When we say we fear something
What do we mean?
Is it an excuse to not try?
Do we let it take us over then blame it for being stronger?
What happens when fear wins?
It is telling us it beat us at our own mission

You see we all come here to do something
We come to grow our souls

There are decisions and questions and doubts
Questions of self esteem and love of self
Those stem from fear

And there is love and joy and hope
Trying and things looking like they did not work out
As they are working out
That is love

Fear tells us things won't work out
Not for us, but they can for other people
The worst fear is letting fear win

We give so much power to thoughts of losing
We fear not getting what we want
So we let fear dictate what we dare to want
We don't think of what would happen if we didn't have fear

Try walking the fear all the way through
What would happen if this didn't work out?
You will find that the fear is always greater than the reality
Of not getting what you strived for
Once the fear is out of the way

The love of what you are contemplating can step in
You will not only try, but you will find few roadblocks

For love is the opposite of fear
Love makes things happen

Fear, doubt, and worry stagnate the soul
Love frees it
When you feel love you feel empowered
Because you are
When you love you don't think of negative possibilities
You are consumed with hope

Fear is only a test, a push, the honing of your soul
When you recognize the truth, fear has little standing
Taking chances lets our soul feel alive

Next time your mind says no
Fight it head on
Tell it fear is not your friend
Fear is not the truth
Speak softly with your love

Fear has only the strength that we give it
We all know fear has never amounted to anything
Love really can do anything
Love gives and does not need to receive
Live in the truth that fear is an illusion
Let love be your leader

Relationships

I Want to Love You

I want to love what I do
I want to love what I eat
I want to love the movies I watch
I want to feel the energy of your love
I want to love you

I want every day to be a good day
Not just one day here and there
I want it to be a way of life

I want life without walls
Without doors
Without maybes
Without doubt

I want to feel you when you talk
I want to know that we tell each other the truth
I want to see your eyes when we speak
I want to walk with you hand in hand
Fingers intertwined, like the life we can live together

I don't need anything from you
I just want you to be present
So that I can be present
So that we can be present

I want to watch love stories
I want to be a love story
I want to feel like everything can happen
I want to see your heart leap
I want to leap with you

I want to ask permission of life
To enter it
To live it
To love it
To feel it

We think everything can only happen so much
Limits, doors, walls, gates, rules
Keep us in place

Then there are bridges, paths, avenues, highways, gateways
To take us to where we are going
And today I am jumping
From the inside of my heart to the outside of myself

I want to love you
And it means nothing more than I love you
No expectations
No what ifs
No conditions

I just want you with your whole self
Doing your best
Sharing yourself
And growing in life with me

Babies of Love

I am finally free to love
I am finally free of the thoughts that take away from me
The ones that give me limits as to who I am
Or that say I am not good enough
Or that my need to be loved is more important than me

Love is a two way street
It must come from both of us for there to be an us
And we both must love ourselves individually
To be able to love each other

I realize now, that we will never be one
If that were truth
There doesn't need to be a me or a you
We can make one, a child between us, a common life
But is more important for us to be different than the same

I used to love and ask no questions
Because that is what I thought love was
I thought that love could conquer anything

But love cannot conquer insecurity
It cannot take a lie and make it truth
Love cannot conquer cheating or stealing
Or change what is done

Love is an action, a feeling that we can be part of a team
When our hearts are clean and our hands are working
When our home is open and no secrets live in it
When our souls feel love and freedom at the same time
When we don't put conditions on each other
To prove we love each other
Or that we have to do everything together
Because we love each other

Love teaches us about ourselves
Love guides us to learn about each other
Love stimulates us to know more of life, of love, of people
Love's lessons are as endless as love itself

Love is without conditions or boundaries
No wrong or right
No win or lose
Love is in a category all by itself
It is not sex
It is not one
It is not forever
It is free will to choose those very things
It can say I am here just because in my heart I want to be

Love is the uncluttered mind so the heart is free to know
That love heals us, love saves us, and love carries us
We are all the babies of love
Wrapped in blankets that we call the hands of God
Our souls are a part of God on Earth
Looking for the purity of Home
Here on Earth

And as we find it in each other
Home is on Earth
Purity lights us
And our truth reminds us of the very reason we are here
To love

Teeter Totter Thoughts

When you can't see eye to eye in life
Which eye is not seeing?
If you can't see eye to eye
It can only mean different points of view
Each eye seeing its own way
And failing to see the other side

However no one can see our side
Unless we see that they too have a view
There are more paths then one
When you discuss both paths
You can find points of agreement
When you find a soul who will learn of your path
You find you are interested in theirs

That is learning
That is teaching
Arguing that you are right
And someone is wrong does not solve
It creates potholes and quicksand
Which would you rather have
Truth or problems?
Speak your truth but also be willing to hear another's

Shout your point of view and it will fall on deaf ears
Remember the next time you are upset
To listen to yourself
And be willing to hear what you don't like in what you said
Then ask yourself, if someone talked to you like that
How would you feel?

If you find you are stuck on your side of the street
Take a walk and look around
Remind yourself that we are participants and spectators
We are offenders and witnesses
We are kind and gentle and harsh and abrasive
We are anything we choose to be

Do we need to be right or do we want to understand?
We all long to have qualities we admire
We can possess them today
As soon as we speak with integrity and candor
And respect another's views
We become all we want to be

We make room for others to see us
And hear us
We get to live in the truth of what is
Rather than fight for what we want to happen
That saves us from having to clean up and say sorry later
Our language and our intention
Paves the way to peace and balance
And we know we have all the parts we need
To be who we want to be

Silence is Language

Once you have stated your point, stop talking
When you are in an argument and you wonder why
Stop talking
Let the language of silence speak

When you want to tell someone how mad you are
Stop yourself and walk away
Come back when you figure it out
Hurtful words are never forgotten
Yet the walking away for a time is

We do not need to find out how much we can hurt another
When that happens everyone gets hurt
Not only the ones who hear, but the ones who speak as well
Everyone pays dearly for the pain
Yet silence is the loudest, clearest language

Stop yourself and walk away
Don't participate when you are angry
Strength comes from finding love in difficult situations
Understanding that you don't want to fail yourself
Or the other person

When you are angry is when you are the most vulnerable
Let yourself know there is something you don’t understand
What does the other person want?
Probably the same things you do

Great thoughts stem from understanding
Higher levels of communication
Come from a willingness to consider
What both parties are trying to say

We look for things that will wipe away our disagreements
We say we don't want to live in anger
Yet when we try to erase it
We cannot see how we got there

Learning to accept ourselves when we let ourselves down
Leads to compassion
Compassion shows us the way to empathy
Compassion is the buffer
Understanding is the shine

Knowing when to stop
Teaches us where to start

Perfection is Love

Remind each other
We need not be perfect
That we are perfect when our intent is clear
When there is mental mud we will get stuck in it

Remind each other that life is not magic
It is truth
It is magical when we live it
Teach each other in song, in love, in dance
That life is for living
Not for avoidance

We are not here alone
We are not meant to know everything
We are meant to share what we know
And everything has a chance to be learned

We are not perfect, perfection is love
If we were perfect, why would we be here?
We are here to live our lives
To find the peace and understanding of ourselves
For perfection is love and love is in everything we do
And when love is present, everything feels perfect doesn't it?

So remind ourselves and each other
That we are what is perfect, we are love
And we are here to feel and to grow
That life is something we come to know
And the learning creates the living
And the living teaches us love
And love is the perfection of all of us

After Argument Truth

Are you happy today
Now that the weather is better in our lives?
I don't like being hurt or mad at you
I love you too much for that stuff
You mean too much to life to sell us short of anything
I mean too much to get scared of you

We all have choices and we are making a choice to grow
I want to grow with you always
Just let me know you care and I will be here
I want our freedom, for each of us and for the us that we are

Never think twice about hugging me or loving me
That is an invitation forever
When I get mad at you it hurts me
It doesn't mean that I don't love you
It just means that I had to be reminded
That you are here in heart

There can never be too many times in life to say I love you
And I do
Just know that we are a team, no matter what we say or do
Stay close to your heart and I will stay close to mine
My life with you has never been more fun, interesting
Difficult, and painful
All the emotions that call us to grow

I love you

The Dynamic Duo

I just felt so happy for you
That I feel so much love for you
That you are here and someone loves you like this
That I love you like this

I thought of your life
And how it came to me
And how it feels to care for you
And that you are cared for in this way

It is really something
When nothing is here
And then suddenly it is
How attraction changes all the circumstances around it

When we love music we search for more music
When we love food we want to cook and share our meals
Because we are attracted to things
We get to find out why

Love and Attraction
Look at the power of them in your world
We cannot control these two emotions
They show up and leave us to decide what they mean to us

And when we follow them
They grow into great moments
And new beginnings
And brighten everything we know

Attraction is the light of our eyes
And love is the action of our soul
They are the dynamic duo
The movers and shakers
The ones that win the race

Get to know the people that attract you
Not just in romance but in life
And trust enough to know it is your guide
Your next step to discover who you are
And who you will be

Emotions are the fuel of us
That drive us to our goals
Doing what we love has no comparison
To anything else we could do with our time here

Meat and Potatoes

What you have in common is your key
What you do not is your acceptance
What you like or do not like is your tolerance
What you do not yet know is your growth

Anyone can have sex
But do we know how to have a relationship?
We all know how to meet each other
Yet do we all know how to stay?
How to compromise when things don't go our way?
To stay and we want to run?

A relationship is our growing ground
To learn to grow and still know we are loved
It's hard to do in the middle of an argument
To be willing to rekindle when we are vulnerable
To be open to love when it feels challenging
We can choose to stay and fight
For our soul, for an us
Love can grow if we work through our fears
It is our acceptance of us
That becomes the bigger us
It is in compromise that we find grandeur

Our lives are meant to teach us to get along
With ourselves
And then with others

That is both the meat and the potatoes
It is the meal
It is the balance
It is not having to choose one or the other
It is living in love as you know it, learn it, breathe it

Our love already exists in us
Yet we wait for it to be perfect
Without working at it

And learning how to discover it
Let yourself find love and you will find you
Without judgment

Fill your plate
And your find life
Life in your heart
Warmth in your soul
And it will touch everything you do

The New Sex is a Relationship

We think it is our bodies
Ask any guy, at least until he is done
Ask any woman on her way to "love"

And then talk to that same person afterwards
What do you feel now?
What we realize, but won't often say
Is that our truths were revealed
For if truth were told, both know something is missing

Who are we?
Why are we there?
With this person?
Why do we want to stay?
Why do we want to go away?
What is missing?
Was I impulsive?
Did it feel obligatory?

Did I think about what this means to me?
Did I think it would make a difference in love?
Or was I too wound up needing something?
What kind of person am I?
What do I want from my life?
How do I want to be known?

We tend to think that sex is love
Sometimes sex and love go hand in hand
But we rarely wait long enough to find out
Sex is often based on lack of love
We don't feel our worth
So we give us away in hopes of finding worth
That is why sex does not heal us
Or keep us together or exclusive

You see sex isn't good or bad
It isn't forbidden or not

We let religion, fear, parents, and our culture
Tell us how to feel about it
We are consumed with guilt or rebellion about it

Sex is an emotion
Sometimes shallow, sometimes deep
We bring children into the world with purpose
Or without it
We have a family or we don't

Our bodies are our partners
When we lose sight of that
It strips us of our emotions
And if sex is an emotion
Then we stripped ourselves of what it means to us
Our bodies need not be hijacked by our minds
Yet at times we let that happen

There is a purpose for sex
And a purpose for love
And the combination of the two
Is the grandest purpose of us

It is not about with whom
It is about why
The only reason that gives it purpose is love
Love is the sense of sex
Love is love is love

When we start saying I like you because of this or that
It is not love
Love is love is love

You see, love is a feeling
And sex is the emotion of that very feeling
There is one emotion we cannot control
It is attraction

Which is the feeler for love
And sex becomes the bonding of it

When sex doesn't include love
Your ego has a day at the races
There you go out of the gate
This is good for now
Let's not talk too much about it
You are a great person, however
I am so busy I can only see you once a week
You mean a lot to me, really
I'm not in a place to be with someone right now
Maybe we should take a break

Then every time you see each other you have sex
And then disappear until you need it again...

You can have sex and leave lonelier and emptier
Than when you walked in the room
Now you know why
We need a connection
We need love
We need the emotions that come from attraction

Sex is not a finding out process
When you are not in love with a person
It all seems like a lot of work or a lot of need

Keep alive your love of self
Know that you can hold out for love
Not for a person, but for love

You see, if you eat all the time, you are never hungry
If you eat when you are hungry
You taste your meal and it tastes so good
And you remember it
And you can't wait to eat again

Marriage Does Not Guarantee Love

How can marriage bring you love?
Or stability?
Or security?

How can marriage ensure that you will love someone
Until you die?
Or in sickness or health?

Can marriage really do all of that?
Can it guarantee love?

Can marriage guarantee partnership?
Companionship?
A good parent for your children?

What does forever really mean?
How can we have free will and a promise of forever?

We have tried to corner love
And tell it that it has to work for us
We marry for a beautiful, honorable, and pure feeling
And then we place demands on one another
And it tests us as to how we will be as partners

Really we're just people
Who come here to live and to love
Who then utter words of promise
Without understanding the ramifications
We are scared to trust love for what it is
So we create a marriage that is a lifelong commitment

Judging by the rate of separation of marriages
Maybe we need to revisit the institution
And revise the language we use to join our souls together
We can say:
I love you now and with you I am my best
You see the best part of me

That is who I want to be with you and with myself
I realize life is filled with challenges
I ask your permission to join you in those challenges
I am excited to live life with you and grow my soul
As you grow yours

I look forward to us bringing children into this world
I trust that we will both build a life of love
And share it with them
I ask that when things are not so great
We come to each other in truth
I ask that when you are not certain of us, you will say
"I am far away from you, why?"
I ask that we remember why we choose to be together
And if the reasons change you will come to me in truth
Not create another reason why

We agree to not blame each other
And to understand that we are souls, and we are partners
And in that partnership we do our best each and every day
Promise that we will honor us even if we are not together
That we always remain examples of truth, love and purity
To us and to all those whose lives are intertwined in ours

I love you and I pledge this to you my love, in this day
For each day is growth for us

The Filter of Love

What does it mean to love someone?

It means you love you
It means you know that the other person is you
That they want what you want
That you share in all of life together
Whether you are happy, sad, tired or sick

What does it mean to care about someone?

It means that you pay attention to them
That you will help them when they need it
That you talk and listen and are interested in what they say
That you know it's okay to not know something and admit it
That you face challenges and don't blame the other for them

What does it mean to live together?

It means you both run a household
Trust each other with money
Respect each other's choices
Organize events together

If you have children together
You raise your children to the best of your ability
And say yes to things that are for the good of your family

What does it mean to love?

That you are willing to understand yourself enough
To understand your partner
To see the best in each other
And become your best for each other

To be willing to learn with an open heart
To feel your heart skip a beat to see each other

To see eyes smile
To feel alive with possibility

Love is the feeling that you are alive
And being alive enough to know it

Oversexed and Underloved

We walk around all day and think about
Who we love, why they do or don't love us
We dress to attract
We watch movies that are filled with sex
We drive by strip clubs, bars, billboards
Telling you how you can find love
Or you will be loved if you use a certain product

We work out our bodies, eat certain foods, watch a sunset
All for love
We listen to music that is happy about love
Sad about love, cheated in love, lost love, never finding love

We strive for love
Look for love
Dress for love
Our house shows how much we can love
Our car shows our worth of love
Our conversations say we are alluring enough for love
Our loneliness tells us we must fight for love
And then we find someone to love
And we are bombarded with the stimulus to love
As time goes on we think we can do better at love

We want new, new, new
We want to feel new love
We don't want to try to make love work
We already know this person
Now we want to start over and know another person
Because the new special feeling of love is gone

It is not gone
It is you that is gone
It is you that stopped giving, receiving, sharing
It is you that decided you would rather start again
Than learn to be on the other side of love

The side that takes you beyond sex
The side that says I have been here long enough to find out
That this person is beautiful when they are loved
That I feel beautiful to be loved with calmness around me
That I don't need the dramas to keep me here
I don't need to flirt to prove I am worthy of love
I don't need to use anyone else to feel loved
I can accept a lasting love

When you want to run away from another and start again
It could be that you are meant to move on
You usually know that right away and stop dating

Yet if you have been with someone for a long time
And you once loved them deeply
Then you do love them
Discover them in a deeper way
Live in their worth of themselves as you discover your own
Live life with them as though they are new

They are new
New to themselves
New to others
And new to you if you can see it that way

We tend to take away the beauty of love
When we get restless
We often get restless because we are feeling a deeper love
And don't know how to handle it

Sometimes we don't feel we deserve love so we look for sex
To tell us we are loved

Sex and love have very little to do with each other
Sex is an act you can do with anyone
And not even know their name

Love is a feeling that carries you in life
Sex is a stimulant and a beautiful thing
Yet we all learn that if you are having sex without love
You can leave a room emptier than when you walked into it

For men sex is proof that he is alive and vital
For women sex is proof of being loved and accepted
Sex is neither of those things
Sex is love's truth
Sex is love's sharing
Sex is the closest intimacy to yourself and another

We have taken sex and used it
To sell everything from gum to newspapers
We use sex to say we are worth something
We use sex to hurt others
We use sex to hurt ourselves

Sometimes sex is paid for
Sometimes sex victimizes
Sex is special when it is with someone special to us
Even better when we are committed to another
In a way that we don't commit to anyone else
We are meant to be partners, not alone
And yet we are not meant to have many at once

Sex is the gift of love
We forget the love part
Yet without it sex is oversold and overrated
Sex is a part of life
A release and expression
A fast moment at times
A slow day at other times

Sex is the story of our hearts
We write that story any way we choose

When we settle for less sex feels like nothing
And when we find love and that love carries sex
Love carries us

Until we can understand who we are in love and sex
We will look for it until we do
That is why so many are looking
All want to find it and grow to greater depths of life

If we look to the outsides of us
We will only find the outsides of others
If we become interested in ourselves
We become interesting people
And we will find love in heart, not in body alone

We know love when we feel it
It is usually the love we have passed by while looking for sex
Don't stop short at sex anymore
Know that when we can see love in others
We have found it in ourselves
No more waiting for someone to notice
People notice those who notice themselves

It is not what you would do in any situation of life
Ask yourself
What would love do?

Sex and the City

What on Earth is being together?
Having sex does not glue us together
Being together is the person you spend your days with
Having sex can detach us from love
It is just something you do for that minute with whoever
As long as you both are attracted

Girl Boy
Boy Boy
Girl Girl
Many at once, one at a time, two at a time, three at a time

As titillating as it may all sound
There is an emptiness that permeates it
And distractions increase to cover that emptiness up

People will say that it was just fun
That it's what keeps them in a relationship
That they love doing it

Yet we are all connected
It is how we are connected
How we are together
That builds our foundations
And keeps our hearts close to us and to others

What is happening is dilution
A whole market of sexual attraction
And the bedroom being worn as clothing
Since the world has become a bedroom

Attraction Ignites

Attraction tells us what to do
It whispers in our ear
It excites us
We let it guide us
To expose us
To remind us
That magic cannot be bought, sold, or bartered

We know when to run from someone or something
We also know when to run towards someone or something
It may not look like it fits into life in this moment
Yet it walks us to the light in the distance
And as we get closer we understand the power of the light

Our chests lift with the feeling
Our faces feel warm
Our souls reminds us that it is there

Attraction
It is our fuel, our light, our knowing

It is something everyone has felt and no one is exempt
Everything real belongs to all of us
Our only job is to trust it and follow it
And find out what it wants to teach us

The Music of Love

One day we wake up singing
Without a prompt or a reason
Without music or noise
Only the excitement of knowing we found
Someone who feels like us

Love is the trail we followed
Learning each other in safety
Letting our ugly find itself
And show it to each other
Knowing it would be okay

We learn ourselves through the other
We knew to tell the truth
When we speak we think of both of us
You and me, we are two
There is strength in numbers
When the two are in truth
Someone to say this works for me too

Love's design is to teach us
To build life with another
To know we are still okay
Even when we don't feel like it
Even when we don’t get our way

One of us is always leading for that’s how partnerships are
Each day is an open conversation
About the story we are building

Love comes with surprises
It is more than we thought it could be at times
And sometimes it’s a challenge

The more we can see of ourselves
The more we see in the other
We are treasures

Just as we are
Love helps us to see
And teaches us to care about the little things

We open the door of our souls
As we open the door to ourselves

There is nothing we could want
If we live honestly
And nothing we can give
Other than our purity to each other

Love is invisible
Yet it is felt in its strength
It is the bond we cannot see
Yet the bond of everyday

Love is not a person, a place or a thing
Love is the emotion that we bring to each day
And when it touches another we feel its power

As many questions as it presents
Those questions are answered
As we discover that love is here to teach
There is one main purpose
To love, honor, and be honorable today

The us we have become
The life we have built with those we love
Gives us love's freedom
To be an us
And still a you and a me

The Guessing Game of Relationships

What is it about relationships that keep us guessing?
Is it that we want them too much?
Is it that we think we have to say and do the "right" things?
How can we be so assured in some areas of life
And not in relationships?

It stems from our insecurity with love
We do not feel we deserve it, or we think it will go away
We aren't sure how love looks or know that we can relax in it
We feel like it takes time for us to be ourselves
Rather than just being ourselves
We judge ourselves before anyone else has a chance to

We know what it feels like to meet someone
Who is comfortable in who they are
And because of that we are attracted to them
They don't have to act relaxed, they just are
You don't notice so much what they look like
You are attracted to their ease with themselves

We think it is what we wear or how we look
And yet one day we are caught off guard and love appears
Our instincts attract us to each other when we are real

When we are not relaxed within ourselves
We try to control our circumstances
With our appearance and clever comments
We try to look secure, but it simply looks like trying

There is much to be said for physical appearance
At least initially
Or a great car, or a nice home
At least until you own them

Then you realize they don't do for you
What you thought they would
A wonderful job is only wonderful if you love it

Yet you are not a game
You are a person
Whose heart is attractive and loving
It can stand on its own, if you let it
It can bring to you all that you want, if you let it
We cannot control with things how others come to us
We can simply be us and attract others who like us as we are
We can breathe in the moments that teach us
To live cleanly
To live life with the lights on
To feel accepted no matter what
Because we accept us

Compassion for yourself is the foundation of your love
And the love of you is what draws others to you
Everyone loves to feel love
When you feel it, you find it

Sex Questions and Love Answers

Sex is not a bikini
Though you might think so at first
Then you get the bikini
And when the novelty wears off
You are looking for sex again

Sex is not visual
Although marketing will tell you different
Sex is all feeling
It is not physical at all

There is one thing we cannot control
That is attraction
Once we are attracted to someone
We start thinking about them
Even though we don't know how we feel yet
We are certain that we want to know more, hear more
Explore what it means to be attracted to this person

If we get past the bikini
We start to wonder, who are they really?
What do they like? Do we have anything in common?
How did we meet? Do we know the same types of people?
We want to know all of this because we're attracted

When you first look at someone with attraction
They are special
They don't have problems
You may not have talked to them much
So your imagination fills in the blanks
And you feel with feelings of attraction alone

Attraction buys time in relationships
The impact is so strong at first that we are blinded
Then we introduce them to our friends
And get reactions that sometimes surprise us
Our friends see differently because they are not attracted

Sex is only part of attraction
Without attraction the sex would not matter
Attraction is what draws us to a person
Yet what we do when we feel it is what matters

Is sex the only driver?
Attraction is what is real
Not the sex
Because after the thrill of sex wears off
You hope to still have attraction

When you are attracted
Alive in the thoughts and possibilities
And present with your soul
You are willing to expose your heart
And the most vulnerable parts of yourself to this person

When you have sex for sex's sake
You will soon find
That sex alone doesn't do it
The bikini is great
But where is the love?
Love always wins
Love is not a part of a picture
Love is all of it
The picture, the frame and the table it sits upon

Love and Get It

Being a couple doesn't mean you know everything
Care about the same things
Agree on everything
And never feel like you can't say otherwise
Being a couple is a lesson of love
It is knowing the other person is their best with you
And that when the other is upset
It is simply the fear that you do not care enough

Trust that the reason for your existence together
Is to learn to negotiate and to compromise
To enjoy and to be challenged
To learn the truth of you in a safe place
And to bring your best intentions forward
And know the best intentions ask for nothing
Other than the truth of you
Which in turn teaches that truth to your partner
Your children
And anyone else around

Having a partner is not just having a man or a woman
It is having a human who wants to succeed in life
Who wants to show themselves to you
That knows that hope will always be alive
And trusts that they will always want to grow
That love is endless no matter what you do

When there is love it builds a culture around it
It builds family and attracts those who want to believe
That life works and is thriving
That anyone can go to the safe place you have built
And share their love
That is called community

It is how children learn that love is possible
The home cooks that meals creates their foundation
It all boils down to love

It reminds us that people are important
Every soul, every partner, every child, every neighbor
Every friend and acquaintance
Without love we are lost
And with it we are boundless, endless, and unstoppable
Love is not glue
Love is freedom

Color Me Red

I love you more every time I think of you
My smile stretches every time I see you
I run to you without thinking

Before I know it I am hugging you
I don't stop to think
Should I do this or shouldn't I
I can't help myself
As love is teaching me itself

I hear myself talking to you
It doesn't matter what we say
It is the love I feel that drives me
That runs the conversation
And all I feel is your love when I am away

I trust that life reminds me everyday
That love is open to me too
Silly as it sounds
There were times I didn't believe that

The beauty of love
Is that it never tells you when it is coming
Or how it will come
Or who it will be
Or why

It just shows up in your life
As it demands action from you
It pushes you to do things that you wouldn't do otherwise
And it makes you laugh easily along the way

Love exposes us
It makes us feel like that big red obvious heart
With the arrow going through it

Because when love is true
There are no worries
As love moves in, everything else clears out

Sweet Valentine, color me red, I am yours
Give me the chocolate
Let's eat something special
Go somewhere new
Let's call it a beginning
Of rediscovering us

Sweet Valentine
Come back year after year
Visit as often as you'd like
I am always here
In the brightness of your light

I Want to Be Mad at You, Do Something!

When you are mad about something
And you can't get yourself to talk about it
When someone asks if something is wrong
And you say "nothing"
But it doesn't go away and you feel no better
You think handling it alone would be best

Time goes on, you are not any happier, you didn't handle it
You are waiting for someone to do something
So you can blow up
And pretend it's the reason you're mad

But you feel even worse because you know
What they said has nothing to do with your mood
The other person receives your wrath
And can't understand your reaction

Did exploding make anything better?
Did you really handle it by yourself?
Or did you turn your hurt and frustration into a war
That only you waged

Imagine if you told the truth from the beginning
You said you were not okay, and explained why
You would have cleaned up along the way
And never had a reason to pick a fight

If someone did or said something that bothered you
And you told them when it happened
You would find understanding in the moment
No residue need be carried

We all love to be spoken to honestly
We respect those who won't dump old hurts on us
It takes accountability to keep your heart clean
It builds strength of character

Others listen with love and understanding
As they recognize that you are being responsible
Not only for you, but for all
Everyone is impacted by our attitudes
Everyone can see who we are no matter what we say

Trying to live as if no one can see you
And expecting others to suffer for your lack of accounting
Is the greatest of burdens
Having to fight the things that teach you
Keeps you from the peace of mind you so desire

Take the time to ask yourself why you feel the way you do
Be willing to tell yourself the truth
Take the time to think about the other person
Ask yourself if you are setting them up to disappoint you
Then be angry at them for it

Speaking in the moment is the peace of our souls
It may not be easy to do, but become willing to do it anyway
Peace doesn't come without understanding
Truth only has meaning when we live in it
And we have felt the hurt of not having it around

If you speak in the moment
You won't have to create a moment
To find an excuse to let go of what you are holding
Speak from your heart and speak with love
The relief is unspeakable

Soul Talking

When something says to walk away and we stay
Or someone asks "what's wrong?" and we say "nothing"
Or something tells us to do it and we don't
Or to stop and we won't
Or to try and we say another time
When we want to say I love you and we wait
When we should ask for help but do it alone

When someone says you look great, and we say no I don't
When we're told we did a wonderful job
And we tell them how hard it was
When someone says we are nice and we say not really

None of that is the soul talking
It is ego taking over the mind
And when that happens, nothing good gets in or out

Yet when our souls speak
We hear the clear quiet voice of wisdom
We tell the truth no matter what
We try even when we are not sure we can
We don't put off what is in front of us
We feel love and tell others when we feel it
We help others and let them help us
We do our best and don't look for accolades

When the soul speaks, it calls us to attention
When the soul speaks, we are attractive
When the soul speaks, we are free to love and to live
When souls speak, they speak to each other

When You Say You're Sorry We All Heal

If we could just say sorry
It would heal us both
If we could just think about why we were mad
It would solve many other issues

We forget that love heals us as much as it excites us
Love is everything
It is our healer, our stimulator, our chance at life
When love is in our own hearts
We are open to touch the hearts of others

If we could just say sorry
We would find out how much we needed to say it
Love doesn't care if you are right or wrong
Its only purpose is to create openings to itself
Love really is all you need
Yet when you don't have it
You feel like you need everything else

Don't leave the package of love unwrapped
On a shelf collecting dust
Let love do what it is designed to do

Love soothes us when we are not sure of why we are here
Tells us the purpose of knowing each other
Teaches us the cleanest way of living

We expect so much from love
Like it is coming at us from somewhere else
When really it is in our souls
All we need to do is take a spoon to it
And start tasting

What You Like Least About You, I Love the Most

When the light of your smile
Shines on my hopes
When your eyes remind me I am seen
When you come to me with love
Every gift in the world is gifted to me

It all feels so simple
And it is simple, if love is left to be just love
When love has to be something
Then we feel like we have to be something
And when love is quiet and there is room to grow
We can be quiet with room to grow

Love teaches
Kids teach love
Friends teach love
Family shows love
Love's words carry the truth
Or they would mean nothing at all

Our words express love
Yet love doesn't need words
If someone told you every day they love you
And they didn't
You wouldn't feel anything
And if someone never says it but feels it toward you
You would still know

Sometimes people show up
And it feels like they had always been there
And they were

Only now we see them
Which allows you to be seen

What you like least about you
Is what I love most about you
Because it is you
It is why you are you
The you that I love

The light of your smile
When it's spontaneous
Draws me to you
Reminds me of how love feels like butterflies

Love is all that
And it's quiet about it
Love is in our eyes
And our words can only try to explain it

When We Speak to Each Other

When we say that we don't want to speak to each other
We are saying we don't care about each other
When we say we do not want to socialize
We are saying we don't care about others
When we say that we do not trust others
We are saying we cannot be trusted

When we say we have troubled relationships
We simply do not know what to do next
When we say we are ill
We don't want to face life for a day, a week, or years
When we say we need a drink
We think we can escape our minds

When we say we want war
We have lost sight that a soul is a soul
When we say there are gangs
We are saying that families have broken down

Is it so hard to come to the table with an open heart
To say solvation
Rather than worry about salvation
To find solutions that include others

Our words affect us and others
Our words show us what our intent is
We can speak with love and it will not result in war
When we do not speak with love that creates war

Love really is the strength that we forget that we have
Since it does not seem as strong as it is
Yet everything serves love
And love serves everything
Using it is what creates more of it
Love is the answer, the key
And the way into and out of every situation

Love is the strength, the reason, and the purpose
Love is the dilution of all things negative
Love is the growth of all things
Love is the soulution
That has no way other than to include all of us

Parts of the Whole

The Only Forever is what has Passed

There is no forever in tomorrow
So smile now
Say thank you now
Dress up today
Call and say I love you when you feel it

You create forever in this moment
Forever is not the future
Free will is the future
The past is past
Tomorrow is tomorrow
Now is now

We work so hard for forever
When it has already happened
We work so little for this moment
When the only moment is now

Hold your child's hand
Say thank you to someone who is nice to you
Look at your partner and think of the beauty you share
Pay attention to what is here, not what is missing

There will always be something missing
What exists is here now so shift your focus
Let what is in our lives be seen and lived
Felt and received, shared and touched
This moment will be forever in another moment

Bring Me a Higher Love

Your higher self is talking
And you tell it what is not possible
That you are not good enough
Or strong enough to be that person

Your higher self says that you are that person
You should at least try
You have nothing to lose
That even an embarrassing moment is worth its lesson

Your higher self is you without boundaries
Your higher self is your capability
That doesn't know the word no

Imagine if we never said no to what we think impossible
There would be no questions without answers
There would always be a way

Capability is to know
Ability is to try
To find out if it is yours to have
Or to let it take you to something else

Your higher self is your purpose
And a higher love lets you see your higher self
A soul that says I will because I can
Anything less is not the truth
Ask and you will find a path, an avenue, or a bridge
To take you there

Crimes of the Mind

We think the person we see or hear about
Who did something bad is the criminal
And they usually are
Since we can all see what they have done

And then there is the voice in our heads
Our own internal criminal
That tells us we cannot do this or that

Because we are not ready yet
We don't have enough time or money
Or know the right people
And we don't want to risk what we have

There is no right time
There is only a ripe time

Many people are ready
And allow an opportunity to pass
We don't need someone else to tell us of our dreams
We know what we'd like to be doing
Yet we ignore ourselves
We don't pay attention to our desires, wants and needs

We say we are tired
Or that something hurts
We think someone is in the way
We blame, we justify, we explain why not

For every day that we shortchange ourselves
We feel shortchanged by everything else

We do things that are just okay
And we're willing to settle for okay
And at the end of the day
We only feel okay

We take away from ourselves
Which is the biggest crime of all
Because no one can catch us and take us to court
Or ask why we are not honoring ourselves

Earth is the playground of the mind
We create our reality and we know it
When we follow our drive
Not only are we able to drive ourselves
We teach others to take the wheel and shift gears
So drive and you will be driven

The only difference between someone who does something
And someone who doesn't
Is that someone did something
And someone else didn't
One day, while they were thinking of it
They started doing it

It's not that they are more talented or smarter
Or more courageous than you are
It's just that they started to walk towards their passion
Once you start something you become motivated
We wait to be motivated before we start
And we wonder why it is so hard to get started
We just had it backwards

Passion isn't so hard to find or to feel
Believing it is possible is the hard part
Do it and you will believe it

Emotional Detox

Instead of saying you can't do this
Try this new thing

Instead of saying you won't go there
Go and see what you were missing

If you think yellow doesn't look good on you
Wear yellow

If you never said sorry for something you did years ago
Call the person you offended now

Does your closet need cleaning?
Just start cleaning it

If you always think you should cook more often
Cook

Keep thinking of going for a walk?
Go and Walk

Keep saying you should have a get together at your home?
Start making phone calls

If there is someone you really love and you never told them
Tell them and expect nothing back

You see it isn't what we are doing
It is what we are not doing
It is what we are not saying
And not sharing

Cleaning ourselves from the inside out
Is to give our soul free reign
Without shutting out the beautiful parts
That you are always on your way to finding

Wash your car
Walk your dog
Pet your cat
Remember to say thank you
And I love you

Say you made a difference
And notice how you do
Let the world you see be seen by you
And the world will find a way to notice you

Our souls are not our bodies
Our souls are our actions
Our love that we take the time to share

Our love is all we have
When we are far away from love we feel far away from life
And when we are far away from life we say we want love

No more saying what we want
Forgetting it is in front of us
We make the choice to postpone, to not speak, to not share

It is like not eating when we are hungry
Because we have free will to make a choice
Try surprising your will
And letting it know how free it is

Never Mind Why, Just Do What's Right

Doing what's right needs no explanation
Just do what makes things better
Say what needs to be said
Consider the outcome of our actions

When things are tough, tell the truth
When things are not, tell the truth

We need not embellish a story to make it more exciting
The excitement is in how much you love telling it
Giving someone a chance to feel that it is enough

Nothing has to be bigger or better to be worthwhile
We don't need a reason to say something
It's so much simpler than that
Tell the truth from your heart
And the truth will do the rest

When you don't want to tell the truth
Ask yourself, why do you want to lie?
What is at risk?
Your self worth? Your image?
Is lying something you want to carry around?
Do you want to create distance between you and others?
Do you not have enough respect for yourself to be honest?
Do you prefer the drama of lying?
Do you know that lying will cause you to not trust others?

Most who do not tell the truth
Always assume others lie too
They don't like to discuss details
Nor do they enjoy the fruits of self accountability

They are the ones who fear themselves more than others
For they know their charm will wear out
Eventually people will see who they really are

They act as if everything is under control
They tell you how great they are
Often by putting others down
To make themselves look better

When someone speaks the truth with their heart
It's heard loud and clear
They know who they are and are comfortable in that

Getting to know another person
Always teaches us who they are in the long run
If they are someone we can depend on
To always tell the truth and to be reliable
Or not

When we hear the truth we rest
We don't wonder what's really going on
We walk away without questions

Does a person bring you peace and joy, warmth and comfort
Or are you fractured with them and whole without them

When something doesn't add up, speak up
We fight for the truth of our soul
By not accepting what doesn't feel right

Our energy precedes us, we always speak without words
Trust in our souls keeps us clear in our purpose
The places we choose to be in truth
Allow us to experience them whole

Unopened Gifts

Finally a day to remind ourselves
To ask the important questions
How do I forgive myself?
That is one unopened gift
How do I have compassion for myself?
Yet another unopened gift
We know we have forgiven others at times
Yet what is forgiveness?
To forgive is to say you don't know something
You are learning
In simply knowing that, you have learned

You see, it is not about forgiveness at all
Forgiveness says that you will pardon
Something another has done to you
Or something you have done to yourself

That simply means you have not learned the lesson
So you will forgive the action
And the residue stays with you
Because you didn't answer the important question
Why did it happen?
To ask is to learn

Compassion says that in whatever happened
We will learn from it
Not simply to avoid it next time
But to understand why we did it
What we thought we were gaining
How did we put ourselves there?

We teach children three rules of discipline to follow
Don't hurt yourself
Don't hurt others
Don't damage or destroy property
That is the simple truth for all of us

If we don't hurt ourselves
We will never hurt others
We become willing to see how we hurt another

Compassion is the next step, the human part
That we all make mistakes
It doesn't mean it was intended

If we say words like
I know you didn't mean that
I can see now your intentions were good
And if they weren't it is a place for me to grow
Or it is not a place for me to stay
Compassion finds a solution
It is how we learn why, not just what
Where we see the motivation rather than just the action

The difference between forgiveness and compassion
Is that compassion teaches love
Forgiveness gives power to someone to grant it

Look for the unopened gifts
Give them to yourself
And you will find a treasure

As the Angels Sing

The angels sing today on Earth
Words of love flow around us
Tears of truth well up without warning
We are open to each other
We forget we live in a world
And remember that we live in one home

We are the love of many touched by one love
When love is pure it propels
When truth is present we stand tall to the realization
That we are our best when we feel all is possible
All we have to know
Is that we believe we are the best of us

We love the love of this day
We love that the world shrunk
That everyone on Earth can say yes to the same thing
For one moment in one time

Time is timeless
It does not matter what year it is
Suddenly nothing matters but the love that each of us feels
Looking at the person next to us and realizing we are the same
We are together
God gave us all fingers
So that we can hold each other's hands

One Size Fits All

We love it when people...

Are vulnerable, because then we can help them
Are telling the truth, because then we can trust them
Are having fun, because then we can join them
Are talking to each other, because then we can hear life
Are healing, so we can cheer them on
Are sharing an experience, as it gives us a forum

Life is about involvement
Of us with others
When we get stuck in wanting things
We forget about others and that we all want the same things

When we are vulnerable and allow others to help us
When we are honest and trustworthy
We invite others into our lives
Which gives them a place to love and us a place to be loved

Our hearts want to join in each other
We all want love
Trust is something we grow
Through truth and respect
And love is the path

Once You Feel Passion You Can Never Go Back

There is nothing to talk about
If we don't think greater thoughts
There is nothing to try
If we are not ignited by the fire of our soul
There is nothing to ignite
If we don't let ourselves feel our love
There is nothing to feel
If we don't allow the love in

There is a lot we think we want
And we wonder why we don't get it
Yet what we think we want
May be exactly what keeps us from truth

When the questions aren't clear
The answers are veiled
When the questions stem from desire
The answers come with simplicity

Taking the time to open your heart
And find the passion
That is our gateway to a life well lived

If we stop at the quick fix
Or at talking about things we don't like
We will never find the things that truly make us happy

It is not that things are possible or not
It is whether we choose to do them or not
We feel our passion
When we take on our desires
Our desires make us want to try

For desire is very different than want
Our desires are not of greed
They are us

Our passion is not an occasional thing
It is constant

Instead of saving passion for another day
Think of it in your choices today
See the difference and you will never go back
Soon you will wonder why you ever accepted less

Passion feeds love and drives love
Passion is the love spoken, the thoughts allowed
The trust you have in yourself
Passion is not letting yourself go
It is letting yourself be

Your Innocence Touches My Life

We forget the power of innocence
We are all innocent in some ways
We see it in everyone we meet
Yet we don't realize it at the time
It is what lingers in our hearts afterwards

It is remembering you telling me something
While you tried to act cool
But you were really excited about it
Or telling me how you felt
And waiting for a response that you so badly needed
But couldn't ask for

Your innocence and your truth brought me to you
We think we are supposed to know everything already
And it leaves us without an avenue to ask
We can be there
Because we want each other to
For our questions and our answers

We are into technology
We are all connected to wires, phones, tweets and bings
Yet nothing that can replace a conversation in your home
A meal that you make and we eat together
A movie that we watch and talk about

Nothing on Earth can hug me other than another person
Nothing else can tell me there is something on my lip
Or that my tags are sticking out on the back of my neck
Nothing can replace me practicing in front of someone
And asking for feedback
We want people over things
We want to live in real time

There is innocence that lives in our eyes
And asks for the things that we don't know how to ask for
We need each other in ways we have forgotten

And what I want for life
Is for life to be shared with the living
To live with people
To see them
To touch them
And know that we need each other

Shouldn't our time be just that
The stretching of our souls
Every day can be just another day
Or it can be bigger
It can be a day for one another

The Best of You

If you can see the best of life
If you can feel the best of life
If you can speak the best of life
You are the best of life

Life is not here to punish you
Life is not here to take away from you
Life cannot do anything to you

You are the stimulus of your own life
No one takes anything away from you that you did not give
No one gives you something that is not yours
No one hurts you
And no one heals you

Healing comes once you understand something
That used to baffle you
Healing comes when truth is around you and in you
Because truth heals

Life is not empty or full
Life is what you create
Life is what you love to do
Life is learning what is in it
Life is giving when you feel it
And trusting when you see it

We grew up with the blame game
But that way of thinking is coming to an end
The economy is reworking itself
Families are redefining themselves
Jobs are readjusting to our growth
We figured out that we fight change
Yet change is why we are here
So let change grow you, teach you, and refine you
Do what you love to do
And do it all with heart

Do it just because you love it
No need to show anyone how good you are
That is what has gotten us into so much trouble
We lost our hearts trying to be something for someone else
Or for image

Live for the first somebody of your life
You
And you will find that only then can you share who you are
Your contribution to Earth is the best of you

The Arrow of the Compass Points to Your Heart

We say we want to hear truth
And then we hear it and get mad at it
And then we fight it
And we think it is fighting us

It is funny when we say we want to be loved
And then someone says they love us
And we fight them
And we think they are fighting us

It is funny when we strive to be pure
And we think we are not good enough to be pure
So we do something that takes that away
So we can prove we aren't deserving purity

If we are interested in truth, love, and purity
Then we will search for them
If we think they are far away
We will find ways to distract us from them

Our hearts and souls are our compasses
If we let our minds drive us to places of lack
We never look at where the compass is pointing
If we listen to our thoughts
We can redirect them
And we can strive for better

Pain tries to deter us
When we know it is simply a challenge of love
We can heal
When we believe pain is in someone else's hands
We allow another to control our lives
And then we feel lost and hopeless

Yet the decision is ours alone
So when our mind tells us we aren't deserving
That only others get what they want

Listen to the voice inside that says it isn't so
Why would we listen only to the voice that says we can't?

Listen to your heart that says
I am here
I will never lie to you or take away from you
I am with you, and when you notice me
You are happiest, even when things don't go your way
Because then you remember that life is just life
And you are just you

I am your compass when you are lost
And any boundaries you put on life
Are only there because you put them there
And they leave when you know
You can live life without them

The One Minute Society

How much worse does it have to get before we say STOP!
We just want to hear something nice!
How much negativity do we have to hear
How much take-your-clothes-off music must we listen to
Before we can ask for some different lyrics in life

We don't have to listen to people tell us how bad things are
We don't have to go to movies that leave us disturbed
To watch people get killed to be excited
We don't have to go to events
Instead of sharing time with those we love
We don't have to eat foods that will make us feel bad
Stop doing the stuff that doesn't make you feel better
Stop saying the things that hurt others because you are hurt
Stop putting yourself in front of the news
Just so you will have something sad to talk about

We pay attention to others messing up
Because we are glad it isn’t us
It makes us feel better about ourselves
To compare ourselves to others who are at a low point

We are better than that
Before you speak, ask yourself
Is it necessary, is it kind, is it true
Sometimes silence speaks volumes

Stop yourself when you are angry and want to speak
Take a breath, close your eyes, give it some time
You are never sorry when you practice restraint

Before you say no, think about saying yes
You are never sorry for a new experience

We put a lot of pressures on ourselves to act in the moment
When time is really not at such a premium
We only make it so

By packing our lives with unnecessary pressure
Doing things that really don't matter
And not doing things that really do

We are scared to tell the truth so much of the time
Then we complain that our needs are not being met
It's no one's job but ours to take care of us
When we do it relieves others of dealing with our sour mood

You will find that life has many things that bring us pleasure
We can fill it with a momentary pleasure or duty
But life is richer than that
The joy filled moments can last longer
If we pay attention to them
We have to say "enough" when we feel overwhelmed
And not sacrifice our bodies and our families
Our respect for ourselves can grow
And then for we have time and space for others

As we learn to use different words to express ourselves
Different foods to nourish ourselves
We begin to see and feel hope

The one minute society is becoming old news
In fifty years we will wonder why we lived this way
Stop saying I don't know who I am
You do, we all do, we simply have to give it some airtime

Simple Words

When someone says something unkind about us
And we hear about it
It hurts our feelings and we react by saying
We don't care what others think
And yet we try to not be or do what they said about us

We do care what others say or think
We feel judged by them and want to change it
Those who talk about others
Are the least happy with themselves
And those unhappy people hurt us

They want to poke and prod at life
So that others will feel as poked and prodded as they do
Which is why we hear that misery loves company

We are susceptible to the hurt they invoke
Until we can call them on their actions
And let them know that the ill will inflicted on others
Is just plain unkind

Use the word "unkind"
"Rude" will make them defensive
And they won't let themselves hear you
Talking about them in turn makes you unkind as well
Simply saying they are unkind is truth
And truth brings light
With no hiding place

The simplest words carry the most weight
When you tell someone they are unkind
It is objective
You tell them that it must be something in them
That is causing them to want to take away from others
We see people sticking their greasy tongs into others
We know we all have grease cleaning soap
It's time to use that soap to cleanse all of us

When you can tell another person "that was unkind"
You show your strength by not using anger
That they expected you to use
You can turn the situation to see it for what it is

Try it sometime
It will surprise the soul whose eyes cannot see
Just because it is truth and truth cannot be ignored

Life offers us a way out of anything
With the simplest solutions
The only way we can see the wall
Is to step back far enough to know that we hit the wall
And then we can walk around it

Same Difference

Every ill that happens is an injury to love, caring, or respect
We are often appalled when we hear of such an injury
It startles us to see that we are failing each other
But even more, we fear such things happening to us
We don't want to feel that we can't control such injuries
So we talk about them happening to others
And feel the emotion of it all
And hope it never happens to us

The truth is that we are all different and we are the same
We are different races, religions, and cultures
Which teaches us tolerance
And the beauty of variety
Then we are the same
We all want love, care, respect, and happiness
Safety for our families and a chance to thrive
The sense we are part of the whole
And the whole is working

Understanding we are part of the whole
Takes away the isolation that breeds insecurity
Understanding we are not alone
Makes us want to participate and to take chances
Life isn't about failing or not failing,
Life is about trying and gaining self respect in our attempts
Whether they worked out or not

To live in the whole is to know that we are with each other
In this huge home
Let the doors and windows be only boundaries of culture
Not limits of tolerance

When we walk outside of our room
We get to revel in another's reality
And see that we all have the same wants, needs, and loves
Just spoken in a different languages
But the smile is always the same

It is all here for us
Let not injuries of love happen easily
For to do so is wasting our time here
And missing the gifts

Addiction

An addiction is an addiction
Whether it is to food, to drugs, to work, to sex
It's all the same attempt to escape the life we are living

First we realize we are compelled to do it
Then we hide it
Then we notice it in others
Then we try to stop it
Which makes us binge on it
Then we quit cold turkey
Then we do it again
And we feel worse than before
Because now we know we tried to stop
But we couldn't stop

We binge again and again
We make ourselves sick with it
We hide it more
We feel punished and we don't ask for help
We live in Hell

We try to raise ourselves to the honesty of our hearts
We know have a problem
Yet we insist we will be fine, that we can control it
Because if we let go and asked for help
We become accountable to ourselves
And in turn to everyone else

We all want to be free
Freedom is when our mind catches up to our heart
And lets us breathe truth into our fear

Since You've Been Gone

A soul is itself no matter where it is
How many people think of a person's soul
We think of a person and their actions
As defining who they are
Yet if we think of a person as a soul
We think of them in a different light

When we lose someone we love
We think of everything they were
We remember that they loved strawberry ice cream
How they loved watching "I Love Lucy" reruns over and over
We remember that they loved our blue sweater
And they cleaned their car once a week

We smile and cry
We want to see them and we cannot replace them
We can only love their memory
And all they brought to us
How much they shared of themselves

If we could think of those alive
In the same way as those that have passed
We would be more in tune to each other's souls
Imagine how we would appreciate our moments
How little we would judge small things
And focus on what we love about each other

We see what we want to see
Look at every person you see today in that way
No soul is replaceable, we are unique expressions
When we recognize love and share it
Then we are whole souled

What Money Has Done to Us

It has caused us to require car insurance
Rather than health insurance
It has given us credit cards that has taught us want
It has told us that some people are better than others
Because they possess it
It has made selling drugs more profitable
Than teaching children

We work for more of it rather than raise our children
It has made things more important than time
It has made homes cost more than anything else
It has reduced care for the environment
It has turned talking into something we don't have time for

We let money take over and it did
It makes us fear not having enough of it
We think it will make us look good
We fight our own families over it
We feel insecure around those who have a lot of it
We think less of those who have too little of it

It creates boundaries as to where we can shop, eat, or sleep
It has taught us immediate gratification
And leaves us with no gratification
It is trying to replace happiness

Yet money is just money
It is not a person, it cannot feel, it cannot give or take away
Money is the energy we put into it

What if we set the quest for money aside for a day
We can bring a lunch somewhere and walk
We can wash our clothes and clean our rooms
We can be still rather than go out and buy something
We can cook at home
We can make things that we would normally pay for
We can forget how much money we have

And think about how much of us we have
And then we can choose life over money
And money will simply be the tool that it is
Not the answer we think it is

Money is a rate of exchange
We came here as we are
We leave without money or things
We are here to live

Money is one of the ways to accomplish our tasks
To keep money in perspective causes us to lose the fear of it
Money teaches us who we are
For we are the same with it or without it

Some people steal it and hurt others for it
Money only has the power we give it
So release the thought of need
And you will grow yourself out of the control of money
Into the flow of life
Money is money and you are you
They are separate and we all know
When push comes to shove
Money cannot buy you love

I'm Just Saying

Don't say no when you mean yes
Don't say yes when you mean no
Don't say you did when you didn't
Don't say you didn't when you did

I'm just saying
When you are mad, say it
When you are happy, admit it
When you need to scream, let someone know
When you want to speak softly do it with all of your heart

Don't walk away from yourself
Let yourself be who you are
No one is perfect
Perfection is love
And with love, everything feels perfect

Don't forget you are here to learn
So learn
Don't try to find every reason not to
So that you never change
Or use the excuse that you are the way you are

Live life don't let it live you
Sit and enjoy, don't wait for someone to bring it to you
We are here to feel, to touch, to do
And if what we are doing isn't working
Change it
We can't expect that anyone will do it if we don't
You can start, you can do it, you just have to want to

I'm just saying…

Stand and Deliver

Notice that you speak
And account for your words
Notice what you do
And account for your actions
Notice how you work
And account for your tasks
Notice that you thrive when you are accountable

Your soul is the person you present to the world
The world does not shape you
Our souls shape the world

Do not let the traps of ego take you on
Stand in your strength
And give your soul a chance to have its say

Stand in your truth
And let the truth lead you
You need not tell stories that carry little truth
Nor do you need to talk of your accomplishments
Your importance, or your uniqueness

You only need to be of truth, love and purity
And you will add to the truth, love, and purity
In the world you shape

The Warm Blanket of Forgiveness

One day it happens
We do something that is not typical of us
And the other person understands
It heals us

When we have the moments where someone says
Why in God's name would you do that?
And they really don't want to know the reason
Or hear what you have to say
Walk away until they can

If we do something that hurts another person
And we think we can fix it, we usually can't
We just have to tell the truth
And each of us has to take our own path
To get to the other side

And as we grow in life we learn that what others did to us
In some ways we also did to others
And the forgiveness that was granted to us
We can pass on to those who have injured us

Trust that we are all growing
If we reach out and touch those we hurt or hurt us
We find that we are a lot closer than we thought

Forgiveness of others
Means that you can forgive yourself
Compassion is the warm blanket of forgiveness
When you need love on days when it seems far away
You can lay under its warmth and rest your soul

Under Pressure

The pressures we feel have nothing to do with others
The things we want have nothing to do with who we are
The jobs we work do not define us
We are who we are no matter what surrounds us
More of anything makes us more of what we already are

The pressures push out perspective
And leave us with no sense of humor
And lots of displaced anger
Yet we can turn it around
When we say yes, I am angry
Yes, I have pressure
Yes, it's a tough day
Yes, I feel too tired

And despite all of that, I can take a moment
To breathe and remember to put things into perspective
After all, it's just Earth
It's just life
There is no end point of perfect equilibrium
This is how life is
Sometimes pressure, sometimes not, always changing

No one can take what we do not give them
When we say there is nothing we can do about something
We are stripping ourselves of free will
Of accountability

We can try something new
We can think and believe and know
That we are the ones driving our lives
And we have the power to choose

If You Let Something Go, Let it Go

Do you still talk about it?
Do you still complain that it happened?
Do you still think about it when you say you let it go?
Does it affect your mood?
Do you judge those who didn't do
What you think they should have done?
Do you talk about the people involved?

Then you didn't let it go
You just added another layer to the problem
Ego is involved in every unsolved issue
Ego keeps the circular thoughts in motion

It tells you that you are not done
Until everyone knows how hard you've worked
How much you did and how little everyone else did
Ego says Me, Me, Me while it looks like You, You, You

Pure intent is if you say you let something go
You did
You stopped talking about it
Stopped complaining about it
Stopped judging everyone and everything

Ego never looks like what it is
It simmers at the bottom of frustration
Of chaos and discontent

If you want to solve something
Solve it and grow on
And if you don't want to solve something then stay in it
But don't say you are done with it and relive it everyday
Cleaning up along the way is key
It is hard to do but worth its weight in gold
Call yourself out on your own behavior
And understand that aggravation is a choice

Clear your path by telling the truth
You will take better care of your soul
And save everyone around you a lot of grief too

It is like food
The better you eat, the better you feel
Or exercise
Just doing it feels good
And even better afterward
The more room you have inside of your heart
The more room you have to feel

Happiness Buys Money

We believe money buys happiness
And that love makes us happy
And when we finally get this or that
We will be happy

In fact it is happiness
That brings us money
It is happiness that draws love to us
It is happiness that reminds us that things are just things
And our happiness is our happiness

When we are sad we draw sad people to us
Or no people at all
We watch sad things
We think that we are not enough

When we feel happy
Everything in life has its place
We make good decisions
And we are balanced

It is not that we have to be happy
It is not that we have to be excited all of the time
It is the gentle reminders that come to us in our days
That tell us why we are here
What we love about life
What motivates us
And on our best days how we look and feel
And learning to sustain that feeling
And not letting the stuff that doesn't work change us

We can learn to let things go
To realize we have a choice everyday
To say yes to our happiness
And yes to the challenges
That we will deal with them
And still be content

Nothing is worth losing our happiness
For to be happy is to be at ease when we are alone
Happiness is the fuel that breathes life
Into everything we do
Money is money and happiness is happiness
Money can't buy happiness
However happiness can buy money

Is Anyone Home?

We can easily say we don't expect anything from anyone
That we can do everything on our own
That we don't need anyone
And then we wonder why we are alone

We assume that no one will help
No one wants to
No one cares
These are the red flags of your heart

We forget instinct, the still small voice within
That tells us what we need
We think we can control with what we know
Yet we refuse to know our hearts
We only hear it when what we are doing doesn't work out
And we ignore it yet again

To let control go is to gain control
To let fear go is to become teachable
To say we need is to say we do not want to be one alone
To say we care says that we want to be cared for

So many of us live with our eyes half closed
Trying to outrun ourselves in a race no one else is running
We work hard for what we have
And then we don't know how to enjoy it

So what if I have a great car and I can't smile?
So what if I have a great home no one visits?
So what? We say to ourselves before we fall asleep alone

Love is the so what
Your life is the so what
Stop taking life away
Let your eyes open and see the whole picture
Not just the picture you want to see

It is not what we think we see that is important
It is to see what we believe
And the more we believe, the more we have to see

Expectation Ruins Everything

We are worth what we love
We are worth taking the risk
And not being scared we won't get what we seek
Sometimes we don't know how to accept
Everything falling into place

When what we are faced with
Is exactly what we wanted
We get scared we won't know how to live in it
We spend so much time getting there
We don't know who we are when we are there

We really don't know how to define ourselves
It was always about getting there
About being on our way to it

And then one day
We feel really happy
For no reason
And immediately become scared it will go away
Because...
Why?

In that moment, we need to take a breath and know
We deserve to have what we love in life
This is what it looks like when we are here
When we don't need anything else
When we don't want anything else
When we are content
To know that whatever anyone does
Isn't to hurt or help us, they are just being themselves

Yes, this is what it looks like
And now that we know what it looks like
We want to be here
To be present in it
To feel it and not be scared of it

Every time we expect anything
We are disappointed
And this time we didn't expect anything
And look what happened

Just tell yourself
Today I am going to feel this, learn this, and grow into it
Think of everything else we could learn
Once we accept that we are okay
Without fear that anything will be taken away

We will feel clean in our hearts
We will be okay with happiness
When we expect nothing from it

When You Devalue Yourself

When you think you are not good enough
That means you think others are better than you

When you think you do not work hard enough
That means you think that others work harder than you

When you see a car that is better than yours
You think they have more than you

When you buy a house and your friends come to see it
You talk about all you want to change
Rather than all that you have

When you go shopping and pick something you can't afford
You settle for a cheaper version
Then you don't value it because it is cheaper

When you marry someone and you get to know them
And the flaws come into focus rather than the love
You depreciate them

With all of that, what do we miss?

We miss a great house, car, purse
They're the ones we have
We miss the person we married
For all the reasons we chose that person
We miss the opportunities to enjoy what we have

Then when something happens
And we lose what we have
We wish we had it back
We would do anything for it

So why not look around your life
In your heart's closets and see what you have
Take what you have out of those closets

And invite your feelings into your home
Think of your life as the best in the world
Because you chose it, you have it, it is yours

Enjoy the moments so that you can enjoy your days
Ask anyone who found out they have cancer today
Or were hurt in an accident
How they feel about what they have

Suddenly nothing matters but their life
Their health, the way things used to be
We are in the used to be
Let's enjoy our used to be
Let's enjoy today

Know Yourself Every Day

Just because someone says you can't do something
Does it mean you can't do it?

Just because someone attacks your belief system
Does it mean you are wrong?

No one knows you like you do

If someone thinks they're unattractive
You cannot convince them otherwise
If someone thinks they can't do anything
They will think you can't do anything
If someone does not believe in something
They will not like it if you believe in something

What matters is what we believe we are
That we share these things with others
If someone tells us what's wrong with us
They are simply trying to give us a piece of themselves

So give back the goodness that you are
If someone says something unkind
Say nothing and walk away
Then they will hear what they said

Trust who you are
Everything comes and goes in life
We gain and then we lose and then we gain again
But who are you in both places?

You are on a mission here
A mission with free will
If you are lucky enough to believe in anything
You already have the gifts of life before you
No one has the answers
Yet we all have the opportunity to hope and to grow
Life is not about what we show

It is what we do
Nothing can satisfy us at the end of the day
Unless we acted with truth and love

Trust that everyone comes your way to teach you
So learn from it
Your job is still there to be done
Your life is still here to be lived
And your love is still here to be felt

In This Moment

It is an honor to be in the place
That teaches us something new
It's wonderful to see the light at the end of the tunnel
Even better to see what will come of it
You weren't sure what to do next
And suddenly you can see...

You can see the other side
The side that plans
The side of optimism
The side that remembers who you are
Your strengths and assets
The side that doesn't listen to doubt

The other side of all the challenges we have faced
The understanding that past circumstances have passed
We grew through them and now they are just a memory

It is seeing the other side that keeps us in balance
To know that everything hard is temporary
There is a tomorrow
We need not live in the what ifs or the doubt
We can simply live in this moment
Not holding our breath until something is over

Wherever you are in this moment
Look around and know that everything is perfect for now
No matter what the moment brings
Tell yourself this is all I have to do
This is exactly where I am supposed to be

So let me be here
Talk to the people here
Sit comfortably and enjoy this meal
Do this work and do it well
Then go on to the next thing

It is not what will happen later
It is the moment you are in
Stop holding yourself back
Enjoy and live in this moment
Breathe in and breathe out
Put one hand on the other
There is a magic in that
And smile

It will rest your soul
Rejuvenate your spirit
And remind you that these are the moments in life
That really do matter
As you matter in them

It is you that creates
It isn't already created waiting for you to walk into it
Take a moment and give that moment life
Give it meaning
Give it you

Each Age for a Year

There are 525,600 minutes in a year
It sounds like a lot and then not very much
We spend most of those minutes fighting something

Fighting our looks
Our work
Our families
Our friends
Our age
Ourselves

We love the joy of birthdays yet we resent our body's aging
We look at aging as a punishment
We think that if we use the right cream
Or add something synthetic, or cut something away
We will look young again
We want people to guess our age
And think we are younger than we are
So we can feel more valuable

We want it all
We want the body
We want the looks
We want the energy of youth
We want to be young forever

Yet it is the experience of age that makes us wise
That gives us more to share
Our bodies don't lie
Even if we try to make them
Our soul is not our body

Sometimes we think
"If I didn't see my body, I wouldn't know how old I was"
Our minds are so beautiful that way
Our gray hairs soften us

What would happen if our bodies didn't slow us down?
It is by design, for it is an unhurried pace
That allows us to give back
Imagine if we valued being an age for one year
And we all didn't try to go backwards

If women didn't think they lost something in aging
If men knew how wonderful they become with the years
Our children would look forward to every stage of their lives
And not think that getting older is a detriment

We all come to be born, to live and then go Home
And yet we cannot give up our vanity to enjoy life at any age
We are so scared to be ourselves
That we have forgotten who we are

The Trail of Happy Thought

You wake up after having a good dream and feel happy
You were smiling when you woke up
You decide what to wear for work without thinking
And you feel free and confident no matter what you put on
You realize you don't need coffee today

While driving to work someone cuts you off
And you think that's okay, they must be having a bad day
You get to work and walk by coworkers
Who are complaining about something
You say good morning and you keep walking

You are light on your feet
Free in your mind
And you don't even know why

It shows us that nothing is required to make us happy
We just feel it and it energizes us
It teaches us that we can make a day happy
By thinking about how good we feel

There are plenty of buttons to push
Some of them are the right buttons
There are days where we can't find the right buttons
It seems that the wrong ones are at our fingertips

Yet we have to remember the effortless days
And know that no matter what happens
It will pass and the ease of living will return

Start your day with something you love
And remind yourself that love can happen everywhere else

Peek and Peak

We are the avenue, the path, the bridge
To use the knowledge that we already have
People don't so much need answers, they need means
The means to create a way to use the knowledge
We already have

That is why we know things that we don't apply to our lives
We think we need a new book, a video, teacher
We are just looking for a way to get our knowledge
To produce for us
To teach us how to use our knowledge

Once we do anything, we have a path to do it again
Saying we don't have time is a way to avoid what we know

We live a lifetime to build knowledge
And find out how to apply it
We already know and have heard a lifetime of answers
We keep asking questions
Trying to find a way to use our answers
Action is motivation
Once you start anything, your mind carries you onward
Trust your capabilities
And your capabilities will in turn trust you

It is in your hands, your soul, your desires
To turn anything into something

Don't ask what should I do
Simply ask yourself

What would love do?

The Thief of Time

It's funny how we see many people in a day
But we really don't hear much
We are running all over the place
Working, running errands
Talking on our phones
Listening to music, watching television

At the end of the day we don't feel heard
Like we were there but we really weren't
Wondering if we made a difference today
Or if today made a difference to us

Did we learn anything?
Did we teach anything?
Did we eat what we really wanted?
Did we take care of ourselves?

If we watched a video of all we did today
Or heard a recording of everything we said
Would we like it?

Life really is what we make it
What we want it to be
What we think it is

We create our own realities
And we are all so different
Yet we only feel good when we are the same
But a step above in our own minds
So we feel a little better about ourselves

When we see someone who knows who they are
We are amazed
How come they are different and survive so well?

We want to know their secret
We want to know how they worked around the normal
And did what they love
And are content in themselves

We underestimate our own passion
And when someone is pursuing their dream
We laugh at them
Because they make us nervous
They challenge us inside
And we watch
We want them to succeed
Yet we hope that they don't
So we can feel better about not following our own dreams

We are amazed that other people overcome their fears
And take chances
And risk what we think is important
And whether they succeed or fail doesn't matter
They are just glad they did it

We let fear be our leader
But when was the last time fear produced anything?
Yet when love is the leader
We watch in awe of its power
Its compassion
How it touches our soul
We are all capable
Our minds know it
Our hearts know it
They just didn't expect fear to take them away from you

Fear is no one's friend
It looks just like the guy in the office who is your friend
And then steals your ideas

The Magic of Mama

It's the first Mother's Day
Without my mom
And her voice is still so loud in my head
It makes me smile
And then I cry
But it soothes me to say
Mama

Just saying mom
Whether we have one, had one, or don't know who she is
It is comfort to our souls to say it
To walk into a home
Where food is cooking
The beds are made
The garden is full
The trash is taken out
And the wash is clean

It is comfort that no matter where you go that day
You come home
To what is, was, or feels like mama

The magic of a soul who only gives
And doesn't ask for anything back
Who cooks with everyone in mind
And cleans for the comfort of you when you are there

Mama is mom is grandma is auntie
Home to others
And love for all

When we say mama
We are saying love
When we hear mama
We all know what we mean

Mama is God's hand on Earth
That is allowed to touch our lives in all ways
And your heart's feeding is knowing
That Mama is your magic
No matter who you are

Life in the Fast Lane

Slow down
Being in a rush makes you do things in a rush
Then you are rushed
With no time to feel it, live it, be it
And you miss the journey

We don't think about what we're doing while we're doing it
Everyone wants the results
The numbers
The money
The outcome

But what about the things you learn from it?
Why you did it
How it felt to do it
What you gained or lost from it

Think of how interesting it would be
To talk about how you did something
Rather than the result

If we stop caring about how we learn
We never learn and we repeat the same things
Always in a hurry to get the same results

We meet someone and we want to get married
We want a job that makes us stand out
We think we are less if we don't have enough money
We think our children reflect us
Instead of wanting them to grow into themselves

What if you didn't think of the outcome for a minute?
Would you be doing what you are doing?
Do you love it?
Is this how you want to spend your life?
Can you even see who you are?

The outcome is only the end of the journey
And the journey is the teacher, the preacher, the answer
Once you know why you do what you do
You can feel who you are
If you are grounded in yourself along the way
The outcome means something different
It is who you are as you learn and as you live

Trust in life
Life is a teacher, not an answer
We each have our own ways of getting to the results
We learn from each other
And we are only bored when we are not learning

Slowing down life
Doesn't mean that you are slow
It means that you are part of it
Something we are all trying to be
Only we are moving too fast to get it

The More We See the Less We Saw

It's interesting that we didn't know what color we were
Until someone told us
How we don't know what religion we are
Until someone teaches us
We are taught to judge things we don't know much about

We decide that certain people don't deserve things
Or they are not worth getting to know
It is usually fear of change of lack of acceptance

We don't change our minds or think a different thought
Because we don't want to be judged
The way we judge others

We want to belong to the group that has more
Yet if we couldn't see
We would only be voices and thoughts without boundaries
Yet because we can see, we rely on our eyes for information
And use that information to divide us

We don't pay attention to what needs our attention
Like our resources
The things that make life on Earth more enjoyable
Like hospitals, schools, libraries, food
We let our sight make us interested in matters of ego
To create a fear-based society

We often don't know what we want
But we know what we don't want
So we spend our energy trying to control everything
Isn't that really what criticism and prejudice really is?

We don't like a political party
That may take away from what we have
We think giving our money will mean we have less
We think giving our time will take away from our lives

Maybe if we saw people as the same rather than different
We would be less afraid of each other
And of life
All that because we have eyes
All because we think we can see

Spirituality is Our Natural State of Mind

What is spirituality?
It is using your natural instinct to love

All the stuff we think we have to learn
To be loving
To be giving
To be fair
To be honest
Is innate in us

The first time we lied
We couldn't look the person in the eye
We felt horrible for doing it
We felt like we got away with something that was wrong
That is spirituality

It is not a way to be
It is the way we are

And then teaching comes at us
Teaching us to be kind so we can go to heaven
Teaching us that we were born with sin
Teaching us we need to do certain things
In order to be loved
As though we did not come to Earth for lessons

We came here to learn
The more rules we have
The busier we keep our brains on what not to do

We focus on what we can't do
Rather than knowing that we can do anything
And still be loved
If we knew we were loved
Would we need to do things that make us feel unloved?

A clean heart is a heart that knows of itself
And a heart that is trying, growing, learning
Wanting to be noticed and loved and cared for
And feeling that it is a part of the world we live in

Everyone on Earth reacts to love
As well as to the lack of love
We all need to feel supported in some way
We are all wired to respond to each other
And all we need to do is pay attention
To the truth, love, and purity of our soul

When we say we believe in God, in life, in truth
We open our hearts to what we have always known

It is not spiritual
Or any label at all
It is the truth of our soul's instincts
To live and love amongst each other
And to grow our souls while doing it

Blessings are not what we have
Blessings are what we feel

Time and Time Again, It's All About Time

"Where did the time go?"
"I don't have time!"
When we think of time
We think of time running out
Not like something we have

We look at time as though it is the enemy
We think we won't have time for…
We think we won't finish
We are racing to a finish line we can never reach
So we add pressure and urgency to our lives

It's tiring to think of time this way
To chase the illusion of having more time someday
It really doesn't matter at all

Whether we are nervous or not
Time is still here
Whether we are happy or not
Time ticks on
Whether we achieve something or not
Time passes

Time will always be here
And while we are here
We can choose to do something or not
Time doesn't make that decision for us
Does time pressure us or do we pressure time?

If you really want to do something
You do it
You find a way

When you love what you're doing you don't even feel time
When you don't want to do something
You can't find the time to do it

Time is just a measurement
We are here to do anything we want to do
So take the time, it's yours to take

Monday Monday

Monday is the day that starts off the week
Many start each Monday with the dread of going to work
Waiting until Friday
Because of the position of the day
We have taken the enjoyment out of it

What if we started by thinking
It's a new week
It's a new day
We would find something to enjoy in the day
Monday could become like Friday
Once we finished the day we could rest

Kids simply enjoy each day
Without regard for what day of the week it is
A week is a long time to hold your breath
So take a moment to think about this day
Let your mind focus on what you enjoyed in it
Like a great lunch in the middle of it
Your kid's happiness to see you at the end of it
The people at work that you helped
Or those who helped you

It just means that you are present
Being present is the greatest present of all
Reserving your happy moments for a certain day or time
Is saying the rest of life is unimportant

Smile, and think as you complete your days
That you can be as you already are
Simply choose it and you will feel a sense of accomplishment

Balance?

Think of what stimulates us
We think of love, we think of food
Some of us have passion for our work
Others have passion for money
We all love different music and places and people
And then we all love the same things

We are sometimes stimulated by things that feel bad
Things that temporarily bring us up or take us down
Artificial foods that impair our health
We keep making it and selling it
And leave it up to consumers to find out if it's good or bad

It tells us that we need and depend on each other
To do what is right so that we can rest assured
That we care about each other
From advertising, to media, to food, to banking, to our jobs
We don't always know if it is good for us or not
As long as those who produce goods make money
They will keep producing whatever we are willing to buy

It is sad that this is what we have become
It is sad to say and sadder to live
Now there is a drug store on every corner
So we live longer no matter what our condition
And we are left with little feeling
We are slowly taking our minds away from us
And our hearts even further

Might it be better to live less days and fill them with more
Than to live longer with nothing?

One is the Largest Number

Do you notice how big love is?
No matter what you do in any given day
All you remember is the love
Who you loved
What they said
What you said to them

Was your contribution noticed, appreciated,
Commented on?
If you felt it wasn't, then you know how to appreciate others
Did you do your best and do it with love?
If you did, then you know how important that is

At the end of the day
Do you ask yourself why you did something
You cared nothing about?
Why you were drawn to it?
And what you wanted from it?

Do you think of the moment your ego stepped in
And caused you to say or do or think something unkind
Did you try to justify your actions?
And then did you wonder why you couldn't sleep?

Do you remember the times in your life
That someone cooked for you
Or took you somewhere
Or gave you something
The feeling that someone was caring for you
Supporting you, loving you

Love is so simple it is huge
Bigger than us
And when we have those moments
And we are conscious of feeling them
We feel how immense love is

A big house is empty without love
A home is not a home if no one is in it
And love is not seen so much as when it is shared

We start the sharing with ourselves
We give, and the giving is returned
So sharing starts with one
One is the biggest number
When we are all included in it

Beautiful Today

Think about money
How when you have money
More opportunities are available
Simply because of having resources
However the bigger price tag
Is not using the knowledge we already have
To do the best we can

When we need the best of us to show up
We scream rather than breathe
When we are hurt we want to hurt another with words
That are never forgotten
When we are angry we risk the self esteem of a child

When we cause discord at work
When we eat something we know will make us feel lousy
When we have some spare time and we should take a walk
But we don't
When we try to prove we don't need anyone

All of these things bring about stress
That is costly to our souls
The stress that hunches our backs
Tightens our necks
Leaves us feeling unfinished
We use aches and pains as the reasons
When we know the real reasons and don't want to admit it

If we realize these costs are not worth paying
We can speak from the heart and feel love for a moment
We can take a walk, step back and breathe
We can take better care of ourselves for a change
We can complete conversations
With truth that leaves everyone feeling clean
Find the love of your heart and live in it
Do not store it away for a rainy day
Every day is a rainy day when love is not present

Love will speak for you and take care of you
And you can become the person you know you are
We are beautiful
Beautiful today makes today a beautiful day

Stop Whining Already!

I don't care about how anyone feels anymore
I care about what they do and what they say
I don't care about what they want from life
I want to know what they give in life
How they live from day to day
Not what they want

Hard luck, bad luck, the luck of the draw
What happened to you doesn't matter
What you do about it does

You tell us who you are by what you choose to do
How you look at things
How you take care of yourself when you don't like
What is happening around you
How much of it you dump on others
Or if you take responsibility for your life

Anyone who blames someone or
Something for their circumstances
Is missing the mark
Why are they choosing to not fix things
Or figure out what brought it to them in the first place?

No one does anything to us
Excuses are a thing of the past
Lack of self accounting doesn't help anyone

If you were alone on Earth who would you blame?
We are each other's gifts, not a source to blame
We have eyes that work
Ears that hear
Hands that hold
And feet to take us places

We forget our gifts
And look for what we think we should have
We envy others for what they have
And forget that they worked for it

We are better than this
We are stronger than we think we are
We are here to flourish
Not to stagnate and blame

Don't let weakness become your days
Don't wait for a special day to arrive to fulfill your dreams
That day will never come unless you bring it into being
Sit with others and let your soul peek into theirs
Happiness is a state of mind, not an acquisition
You are whatever you think you are
You create your world
It all begins or ends with you

Charity's Soulstice

Charity touches many lives
Organizations reaching out to people
Charity has become the focus and the hope of us all
Where the ones who have time and means organize
Those who give service have an outlet
Those who need help have a chance

Then there is the charity of our souls
Which sometimes feel that no one is around
Yet when we need it we can see it
A smile from someone makes us feel welcomed
A door opened for us makes us feel noticed
When someone says a simple hello
It can turn us around in a moment
We feel loved

The charity of us is knowing we can live together
Charity is proof of that
Love can be felt in it
To know there is a cushion even when we don't need it
Just knowing it's there brings comfort to our soul

When someone says "you can do it"
You suddenly can
You have a path built on the kindness of another

The first act of charity is from us to ourselves
We give ourselves a cushion
By listening to our ideas and thoughts
Knowing that they matter

The cushions of charity give us the springboards of life
Giving back is an act of kindness
Learning to receive is the other side of love
Charity is a way of thinking, a mindset that we all have
You can do it for you and then you can do it for another

It is no longer for family alone
Family understands it needs the neighborhood
The neighborhood understands it needs the community
The community understands it needs the state
Then we understand that we all matter

Charity starts in the heart before it becomes an action
You can do it
And it will carry many if you do

Blueprint for Life

We need
A political party that represents both the poor and the rich
Credit cards that are not designed to keep you in debt
Contracts that are simple and clear with no fine print

We need less pressure in a day
And more time to work, sleep, eat, and sit with your family
We need to complete tasks without so many steps
To have a doctor to see without permission
To buy all the food that we need
To have books to read and the time to do it

We need to build our neighborhoods
So they become communities
To know our neighbors and spend time with them

We need leaders we can depend on and trust
Jobs we can grow in
Homes we can keep forever if we want to

We need streets that we all keep clean
Parks our children can play in without fear
Homes that aren't behind iron gates

We need clean water to drink
Food that is pure
People not living on streets
Care for those who cannot care for themselves

We all need to stop the blame
Everyone must take responsibility
For those who need and for those who have

To know it is good to get ahead
While still being concerned for others
That people who need help are not to be passed by
And those who need help also must want to help themselves

We need to not accept what is not working
We need to reject loyalty to any party
And grow loyalty to us

People are a party
People are a race
People need food
People need homes
People need learning institutions
People need each other
People need love

There is no soul on Earth more important than another
When we believe that anyone isn't worthy
Of what all people need or want
Then we have lost already

There is no them, since everyone is a them
There is only an us and we all share Earth
It includes people, animals and nature

When you find something to complain about
Look again and find something you can do about it
That is balance
Pick up trash that you see
Smile at another and remind them we are all here
Remember that there is no way to do this alone
Leadership cannot work without people
People cannot have order without leadership

We each have a job to do
Yet we spend so much time trying to not change
We think the good times are past
Yet nothing is meant to stay the same
All is meant to evolve

It is simply important that you notice
Anything can happen
We are one
Everything has a blueprint and we are the blueprint of life
Awareness is how we know what to do
And love is the fuel of it all

Love is our leadership
Love is our search
Notice love and you have already begun the movement
The movement of living life as you dream it
And dreaming it as your life gives you answers
And answers keep you thriving for more

Think of Earth as a Dream

In a dream things magically change
You fix things miraculously
You get out of situations and don't know how
You feel energized when you wake up
And you don't even remember all the details

Dreams are journeys
Where we get to do things we only dream we can
Even if we haven't done the things we dream about
We feel like we actually could
That what we thought wasn't possible is

Dreams are the options
The visual pictures to our thoughts
Our dreams tell us what we can do
Yet when we wake up
We dismiss the dream as just a dream

Dreams are simply spring boards
What you saw there you really have done in a way
So when you are thinking, I would really love to do that
Say, why not?

There is nothing to lose in thinking you can do
What you dream
Dreams occur when we are too far away to stop them
Imagine if you dreamt those dreams awake
That is called reality
When you let your dreams come alive

Dreams are always there, so pull them in a little closer
Draw them into you
From there to here

A New Day

What if the New Year gave you everything you wanted?
What if you knew everything you ever wanted to know?
What if you knew that you were financially stable?

What if you knew nothing could hold you from your desires?
What if everything was perfect in your life?
What if you knew you could do whatever you wanted to do?

Feel what it feels like to know those things
Write down a list of the things you desire in life
Now find a way to achieve them
Stop thinking of the reasons why you can't

Write the first thing down you would do to begin
Write the second thing you would do
Keep going until all the steps to your goals are covered

How would you like to see your family?
Write it down
How would you like to be employed?
Write it down
How would you like to see your health?
Write it down

Now do it. Start right now. Not tomorrow. Right now.

How are your relationships?
Is there anyone to whom you owe an apology?
Do it now
Do it by email if you want and don't expect anything back

You see when you set goals, you achieve them
When you aim at nothing, you hit nothing
If you keep doing what you've always done
You keep getting what you've always gotten
So try something new

When you achieve your goals
You have just taught others how to do it
When you give to your family, your work, and your health
It breathes life into everything around you

The New Year isn't about starting a new diet, a new job
Or anything else that is new
The New Year is a time to take inventory
And change the life you are already living

You are bigger than the life you are living
So start moving up
You cannot do anything without starting

Think about the things you have written down
Picture yourself doing them
Feel what it feels like to know it is already done
Take action toward starting it

Put everything you have written in an envelope
And put it away
Open it one year from now
You will be surprised and you will learn to trust
That you can do anything you set your mind to

Happy New Year, this year and the next and the next
It is the new habits of the New Year
That keep it new all year long
You won't need to see fireworks because you will feel them!

Spirited Thoughts

Love is objective

The worst truth is better than the best lie
Lazy souls, wilted dreams
Superficial is the blocking of the sun
Whatever it is, just say it, even if it is only to yourself
Not understanding yourself leads you
To not understanding others
Not understanding yourself leads you
To glamorizing others
Not understanding yourself leads to
Thinking everyone else is better than you
And your goal becomes to be better than them

Taking responsibility for your actions is the best any of us can do
Living in the moment is a gift and you know it when it happens
When you trust someone or something, you really relax
Food always calms everyone
Sharing food brings people together
Saying hello to anyone breaks the ice
Helping someone melts the ice
Fear is the plug we can pull anytime
We spend our lives looking for love
Better to find the love that is already in your life and live in it
And more love will come once you recognize the love you have

Trust in life gives you the freedom to think of other things
Traveling makes you appreciate home
Home is your heart's content
Leave the door open and allow life to visit
When you need quiet

Close the door for a day or two then reopen for business
Because a business only thrives when it is open

Free Will

Free Will is the Key

When we don't like something
We say we want to change it
While we continue doing the same thing
Waiting for that moment to start anew
As though that moment has to come to us
We almost demand that it does
Because change is supposed to happen naturally, right?

Then frustration sets in
Because we are waiting for opportunity to show up
Rather than create something in the time we have
We think that we are supposed to do things a certain way
And we forget the options, the new ideas
The ones we can only find if we open our minds

No one can give to you what you cannot give yourself
And you can only share what you have figured out
Remind yourself of the last time you followed your intuition
How the outcome didn't matter
As much as what you learned along the way

Decide you can do something different
And it will already be done
All you have to do now is physically do it
It is truly a matter of will

Let your free will be your guide
It will teach you to have truth
It will teach you to trust
It will never lead you astray
Free will is the reason we are here
When we forget that
We really do forget why we are here

The Magic of Us

The magic of us is the beginning of learning
That teaches us to walk through the middle
And sustain to the end
The magic is knowing how to finish
Our thoughts and actions
To examine motivations
To be interested in truth

The magic is enjoying the fruits of the trees we have planted
Knowing there are no mistakes
If we find ourselves somewhere, we were meant to be there
Knowing that learning is why we are here on Earth
At times learning won't be easy
But it is always worthwhile

The magic is knowing we have free will to choose
The paths of our learning
We want to make the best choices for ourselves
And for those around us
Yet whatever choice we make it is just another avenue
To yet another learning

For we are souls who can speak and do as we wish
The magic is understanding the desires of our souls
Not spending time thinking of what we cannot do
Or do not have
As if we have no choice in the matter

What we can do, if we choose to, is so much more
Free will is ours to use
It is free to guide us
Our free will is the magic and the magic is free

Free Will

There is no promise, no means, no future guaranteed
For free will is the truth of Earth

On Earth souls want something to hold onto
To know what is coming
To feel better and better and better
Yet when they feel better
There is always something else that tells them
"You will feel better after
You get, do, or achieve this or that"
And until then, you are in the on your way
To "feeling better" mode
Feel better than what?
Feel better and then what?

Feel good in the moment
You will be in your truth
The moment that you are living
Is the moment of truth, your truth
What are you doing now?
For that is who you are
Who you chose to be
Why you are
And why you chose it

Souls are so lonely inside
They want and want and want
For they want to fill that loneliness

Souls forgot so much
They forgot that they need each other
Without expectation of why they are with that person
Or job, or have what they have

For if there was love, pure love
These questions would not come to mind or heart
A soul would then know why

There is so much confusion as how to feel
Free will is the leader of all living
We are from each other and of each other
Yet we are not each other
What would the point be if we were all the same?
It could not be
For then there is purpose

No learning, no growth
We all have the same constant
The variable is our soul,
Our perceptions
And how it is that we grow in love

Free will is what differentiates us

For no soul is stuck
Some will fight you to the ground
As they assert that they are not stuck
Ask souls to ask of themselves
Why it is that they want to be here
To do this, to be stuck?

You got yourself stuck
For self accounting has gotten so far away
That there is no responsibility for the creation
Of soul's realities unto themselves

Which things of your own doing contributed to your life?
What was involved?
Your desire for what?

For money, for fame, for recognition
For a perceived perception of yourself?
For relief of pressure?
For the fulfillment of Ego at any level?

Souls are wondering why they even exist
Let alone what they are to do here
Waiting for someone else to tell them
Ask yourself
In my grandest of dreams what is my ideal of life?
Find a way to do it, for that is you
For the loss of dreams gave free will a punch in the face
That it has not recovered from yet

A soul can choose to believe or not
To say love does not exist
To say that there is no love
That souls cannot be pure
And as long as this is said it will be
For that is free will

Free will creates all that exists around it
Nothing else
That is how powerful free will is
Free will is the playing out of the soul's desire
To manifest and become and so it does

There may be a soul who wants to stay with another
For feelings of guilt or stability
And then they stagnate
However free will is open to all souls
The growth of a soul is to find
What the world gives to it to learn
Or it can stay and question itself for the rest of its life
That is free will

Another soul may say
I do not know how to accept love
And free will listens intently
And they will indeed not know how to accept it

If a soul says
I won't be happy unless I have this or that
Do this or that, whatever it is
It will be that the soul will only be happy
Unless and until it learns

That putting conditions of love and happiness
Is not an unless...it exists regardless

So many souls are hung up on who they are
If they are
That they cannot hear any better
Than the soul who is saying
I will only love me if or when this or that happens
Until I know all the facts then I can really believe

Love is still here while souls spin their reasons
As to why it is not
The only difference is that
They do not partake in love for that very reason